PRIMARILY WRITING

*A Practical Guide for Teachers
of Young Children*

PRIMARILY WRITING

A Practical Guide for Teachers of Young Children

Debbie Rickards

and

Shirl Hawes

T 11809

Christopher-Gordon Publishers, Inc.
Norwood, Massachusetts

Copyright Acknowledgments

All student work used with permission.

Christopher-Gordon Publishers, Inc.

1502 Providence Highway, Suite #12
Norwood, Massachusetts 02062

800-934-8322
781-762-5577

Printed in the United State of America
10 9 8 7 6 5 4 3 2   07 06 05 04

ISBN: 1-929024-52-5
Library of Congress Catalogue Number: 2002112041

To Kelsey and Michael

D. R.

To Hawsey, Ali, and Josh

S. H.

In memory of Robert J. Arbs and Dan E. Worcester

Contents

Acknowledgments

We owe a large debt of gratitude to our friends and colleagues who have helped us in our long professional journey to this book. Here are just a few of the many people who have strongly influenced the creation of this work.

We appreciate the collegiality of the district and school personnel who have made our teaching enjoyable. We are thankful to our school districts, Alief Independent School District and Fort Bend Independent School District, both in Houston, Texas, for their support of us as professionals. We are especially indebted to our colleagues at our schools, Boone, Rita Drabek, and Arizona Fleming Elementaries, for their encouragement and friendship.

This book could not have been written without the wonderful students that we teach. Many thanks to the primary students at Arizona Fleming and Boone Elementary for the lessons they've taught us. We have tried to capture a small part of the many joyous and amazing efforts of these young writers.

We are most fortunate to have the support of exceptional friends and colleagues who have helped us to refine our thinking about raising young writers. We are especially grateful for the contributions of Cindy Cecil, Deb Diller, Crystal Hildebrand, Megan Hutchison, Georgia Nemeth, Suzy Price, Ron Robinson, Kathy Spiech, and Dawn Westfall as we've refined this text. We offer a large debt of gratitude to Cookie Lancaster for her careful editing of our manuscript.

We would like to express appreciation to Paula Groberg and Kathy Stuart from Baytown, Texas, who inspired us with their "Read, Write, and Rock Like a Rainbow" presentation at the Texas State Reading Association Conference in 2000. These women helped us to reconsider our instructional format for writing, which resulted in the development of VOICES (explained in chapter 4).

Our relationship with Christopher-Gordon Publishers has been a supportive and enjoyable one. We're especially grateful to Sue Canavan, executive vice president, for her assistance and encouragement.

We must acknowledge our mentors, whose professional writings have made such an important impact on our teaching. Sincere appreciation is due to Carl Anderson, Lucy Calkins, Ralph Fletcher, Marcia Freeman, Mary Ellen Giacobbe, Donald Graves, and Regie Routman for helping teachers to envision what could be.

We could not have reached this professional position without a firm foundation. We acknowledge and deeply appreciate the contributions of our parents, Martha and Robert Arbs, and Betty and Dan Worcester. They always had faith in our abilities, supported our professional efforts, and took pride in our achievements. It was their nurturing and love that helped to make our professional work possible.

Most of all, we are profoundly thankful to our families, who have offered constant love, support, and patience. Words are inadequate for expressing their contributions to our professional and personal lives. Thanks, Dan, Hawsey, kids, and grandkids, for making all our dreams come true.

Introduction

The art of teaching is the art of continuing to learn. Teachers are the most important learners in the classroom.

—Donald Graves, *A Fresh Look at Writing*

We, Debbie and Shirl, are learners. As teachers, mothers, wives, friends, and homemakers, we place learning as a high priority in all our endeavors. We strongly believe that we are the most important learners in our classrooms. Without our personal focus on professional growth, our teaching practices would have remained firmly grounded in the 1970s. Heaven forbid!

In the 1980s, we both transformed our writing instruction, in large part due to the revolutionary work of Donald Graves, Lucy Calkins, and Mary Ellen Giacobbe. Since the birth of writing workshop, we have continually honed our teaching practices. This book represents our current level of understanding about what makes an excellent primary writing program. It was written mainly for primary teachers, but we believe that all elementary teachers can benefit from much of the information in this text. Our intent is to provide explicit instruction and explicit examples from our own practice. We know that as learners we will continually strive to perfect our teaching to meet the needs of our young writers. We encourage our readers to do the same. Try the lessons suggested here and then adapt the work to make it your own and to meet the needs and interests of your particular students.

Although this book is quite comprehensive, we don't address some issues that relate to writing instruction. We've given you just a little information on implementing a writing portfolio system, and we haven't addressed the role of technology in a writing program at all. We've intentionally omitted both topics—there is enough information in this text to keep you busy!—but there are many other resources available if you want to learn more about them.

So that we all can continue as learners, we've developed a Web site to share new understandings and instructional ideas related to primary writing instruction. We invite you to visit the site, www.primarilywriting.com, to learn new teaching ideas for young writers and to share your own experiences in developing an excellent writing program. Many of the forms offered in this text are also available on our Web site.

We welcome feedback from you as you move from competence to excellence in your teaching practices. Good luck as you raise exceptional young writers!

Chapter

1

Raising Young Writers

Focus on the writer and the writing will come.

—Mary Ellen Giacobbe, quoted by
Donald Graves, *A Fresh Look at Writing*

"Can I bring my writing out to recess, Ms. Rickards?" Lakesha asks Debbie at the end of their daily writing workshop. "I want to work on adding some more details to my words and illustrations."

Across town in Shirl's classroom, Jose inquires, "Can we have a conference about my lead, Ms. Hawes? I need to talk about my choice of words."

These two primary students have been raised in classrooms that nurture young writers. Just as parents raise their children to reflect their beliefs and values, teachers of young students have a powerful impact on the beliefs and values of their students about learning. We believe that it's imperative for students to see themselves as readers and writers at the earliest opportunity—kindergarten, first grade, and second grade. In this way, students develop habits of thinking about literacy that will sustain them through later grades. One way to help our primary students view themselves as writers is to raise them in an environment of a daily writing workshop.

This book was written to share our experiences as primary teachers as we have journeyed to become better teachers of writing. Shirl has worked and refined her teaching skills almost exclusively in the first grade. Debbie is currently a literacy support teacher, working with teachers to expand their literacy instructional practices. She has taught both first and second grades and has conducted writing workshop in kindergarten as well. Both of us teach in classrooms where many of the students have limited literacy experiences, receive free or reduced lunch, and come from families that speak a language other than English. Our students range from gifted to seriously at risk. What we share here are a few of our successes as we've tried to raise the young writers in our classrooms.

Why Writing Workshop?

In the examples above, Lakesha and Jose help us to see the power of a daily writing workshop. Their motivation for writing is obvious; they are both eager to spend their time working on their written pieces. They effortlessly use the language of authors. Both see revision as a natural and necessary part of writing. Unquestionably, Lakesha and Jose view themselves as authors, and they avidly approach writing as an integral part of their daily routine.

We think Regie Routman (2000) says it best:

> Writing is the best tool I know for thinking, communicating, and discovering. Writing allows us to consider and reconsider ideas, positions, statements, and thoughts; to hypothesize, problem-solve, challenge, argue, create, summarize, ruminate, ponder; and to have a record of all this thinking and creating. Writing encourages us to question, reflect on our thinking, read about other ideas and perspectives, change our minds, reach for loftier goals. And when we write we do all these things simultaneously. (p. 206)

In short, writing is thinking.

The Importance of Reading Aloud

Could you write a cookbook if you'd never done any cooking? Would you consider writing a college textbook about nuclear physics? We doubt that you'd try either task because your lack of experience with the subject matter would make the writing difficult, if not impossible. By the same token, our students require lots of experiences before they write. Not only do they need experience with subject matter, they also need to understand features of different genres before expanding their repertoire of topics.

In her book *Read to Me: Raising Kids Who Love to Read,* Bernice Cullinan (1992) offers numerous reasons for reading aloud. She asserts that children who are read to experience the following advantages:

✓ They have fun.

✓ They build the desire to read.

✓ They have an educational advantage.

✓ They establish loving bonds with the reader.

✓ They develop vocabulary.

✓ They develop understanding of other people.

✓ They develop the ability to read alone.

No primary teacher we know would argue with these advantages. Unfortunately, we seldom consider the benefits that reading aloud has on writing development.

The first necessary element of a successful writing program is an abundance of read-aloud opportunities in a variety of genres—fantasy, realistic fiction, informational text, poems, how-to pieces, letters, and so on. These read-aloud experiences help students to develop an ear for the attributes and qualities of different genres. Shirl has a routine that helps to ensure that her first graders have a range of experiences with read-alouds. Every day, Shirl reads a variety of literature that includes one chapter from a chapter book of her choice, one book from an author study set, several poems, short sections from a nonfiction text and a biography, and a picture book that corresponds to a comprehension strategy. (See *Strategies That Work* [Harvey & Goudvis, 2000] and *Reading with Meaning* [Miller, 2002] for more information on teaching comprehension strategies.) In addition, Shirl makes sure that her read-aloud selections are multicultural and honor the diversity of students in her classroom.

As students become familiar with many books from a specific genre, the opportunity to analyze these texts is now present. You and your students can discuss the features of a particular genre, the qualities of the writing that make the book enjoyable or interesting, the strategies that the author may have used, the support that the illustrations provide, the connections to other texts, any questions about the book, and so on. These discussions help to prepare your students as they become authors themselves. For example, if you want your students to write fictional pieces, they must first have a solid understanding of the characteristics of fictional story elements (characters, setting, problem, events, and resolution). If you are targeting nonfiction writing, your students must first be thoroughly familiar with the purpose of nonfiction (to inform), its various text structures (e.g., comparison-contrast, cause-effect), and its features, such as captions, headings, boldface type, and labeled diagrams. They become familiar with these aspects of texts through read alouds, analysis, and discussion. We'll explore this idea further in chapters 3–6.

Daily Writing Workshop

We can't stress enough the importance of a *daily* writing workshop. Children (and adults!) become more proficient at writing by practicing often. To improve our writing, we all need time to experiment, try new skills, mess up, delete, start over, share, and revise. In addition, children need to visit their writing daily so that they can sustain interest in one topic. They lose momentum if they only write once in a while. Most important, however, is the underlying message you send when you schedule writing workshop as a daily part of your classroom routine. It says to your students, "Writing is important. I value writing. I want you to value writing, too."

Writing Workshop Format

Devoting an hour a day to writing workshop would be ideal. Forty-five minutes would be wonderful. We realize, however, that time is one of our most precious

Table 1-1.   Debbie's Second-Grade Daily Schedule

7:55–8:00	Announcements
8:00–8:10	Morning business
8:10–8:30	Calendar
8:30–9:40	Guided reading/Work stations/Sustained silent reading
9:40–10:00	Shared reading
10:00–10:10	Morning break (bathroom/snacks)
10:10–10:45	Writing workshop
10:50–11:50	P.E., music, or art
11:55–12:15	Word study
12:15–12:45	Lunch
12:45–1:15	Read aloud
1:15–2:00	Math
2:00–2:50	Science or social studies
2:50–3:00	Ready for home
3:00	Dismissal

commodities. Neither of us could ever chisel out more than 30--40 minutes for writing workshop on a daily basis, so we'll discuss a writing workshop format based upon that amount of time. If you're lucky enough to find more time in your daily schedule, we recommend that you use the extra time for children to work on their writing. Table 1-1 shows Debbie's daily schedule, and Table 1-2 outlines Shirl's. Although our schedules show specific times for each content area, in reality the times are used flexibly, depending on the activity. In addition, other writing opportunities occur throughout the day in all content areas.

Table 1-2. Shirl's First-Grade Daily Schedule

7:50–8:00	Morning business
8:00–8:10	Announcements
8:10–8:30	Treasure books
8:30–8:50	Shared reading
8:50–10:00	Guided reading, work stations, sustained silent reading, partner reading
10:00–10:15	Word study
10:15–10:30	Read-aloud: Author study or comprehension strategies
10:30–11:00	Lunch
11:00–11:30	Recess
11:30–11:50	P.E., art, or music
11:50–12:05	Read-aloud: Chapter book, poetry, biography, and nonfiction
12:05–12:45	Writing workshop
12:45–1:00	Calendar
1:00–1:45	Math
1:45–2:25	Science or social studies
2:25–2:35	Ready for home
2:35	Dismissal

Writing workshop begins each day with a mini-lesson in which the teacher helps students to focus on writing skills and strategies. The time devoted to the mini-lesson varies, but it generally averages about 5 minutes. The mini-lesson is followed by a longer time for sustained writing. During this time, students are writing independently, sharing with a partner, conferring with the teacher or peers, or participating in small group lessons. Writing workshop ends with an opportunity to share. Table 1-3 illustrates a typical writing workshop schedule.

Table 1-3. Writing Workshop Format

5–10 minutes	Mini-lesson
20–25 minutes	Sustained writing, conferences, small-group instruction
5 minutes	Sharing
TOTAL = 30–40 minutes	

Using Children's Literature

We've talked about the importance of immersing children in an abundance of read-aloud opportunities to help them develop an ear for the different genres they'll be studying. Children's literature has another benefit as well. By examining well-written trade books, teachers can help students to focus on the many qualities of good writing. For example, Judith Viorst's *I'll Fix Anthony* (1969) is ideal for helping students to understand voice. *George Shrinks* by William Joyce (1985) helps students to understand how illustrators make sure that the illustrations match the text. For showing students how authors describe setting, *Tar Beach* by Faith Ringgold (1991) is an excellent choice. More information on using children's literature is available in chapter 3.

The Importance of Modeling

Children's books provide wonderful models for writing. The most powerful model, however, is you. Throughout the school year, you will write in front of your students. You will model topic selection, planning, revising, editing, and all of the target skills that you want your students to learn. You may feel uncomfortable at first; initially we both felt awkward and still are sometimes self-conscious as we write in front of our students every day. We encourage you to overcome these feelings. The modeling task will get easier for you, we promise, and your students will reap the rewards of having a teacher who clearly demonstrates what writers do as they compose a text.

Gradual Release of Responsibility

The gradual release of responsibility model (Pearson & Gallagher, 1983) shown in Figure 1-1 illustrates how your modeling changes over time. When introducing a particular writing skill, you assume full responsibility for its implementation as you model the skill in your writing. As you continue to write in front of your students, you will still model the specific skill, but you will also assist students as they use the skill in their own writing. Finally, the skill becomes so habitual for students that no further support is needed. The student then assumes full responsibility for using the skill in his or her own writing. This gradual release of responsibility sustains young writers as they work to apply the lessons that you have modeled and supported.

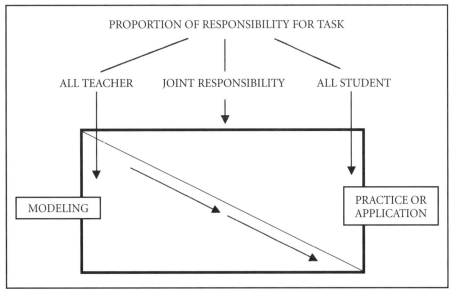

Figure 1-1. Gradual Release of Responsibility

The Teacher's Role

The teacher serves the following functions during writing workshop:

1. Model
2. Coach
3. Planner
4. Diagnostician
5. Consultant

Of primary importance is the role of model. You'll write in front of your students, revise, edit, and think aloud. As students write, you'll serve as their coach. Just as a football coach motivates the players and helps them to apply skills and strategies appropriately, you'll do the same for your young writers.

You will also be a planner and a diagnostician. You'll utilize the skills and objectives mandated by your state and district curriculum guides as you plan your instruction, but you will also be diagnostic about your planning, basing instruction on the needs of your students. You'll plan for both whole-group and small-group instruction. To be a better diagnostician, you'll assess the progress of your writers using a developmental continuum or rubrics based on the skills and strategies you've taught (see chapter 8).

Finally, you'll serve as a consultant. You will consult with your students about their writing, both individually and in small groups during conferences (see chapter 7). You'll give compliments, critique, nudge students to apply writing skills and strategies, and urge them toward deeper understandings of writing techniques. You'll be the mentor who can help students to develop habits of thinking about writing that will sustain them as they mature in their writing abilities.

Mini-Lessons

As you conduct writing workshop in your classroom, you will design mini-lessons based upon the needs of your students. Mini-lessons are brief coaching sessions in which you help students to develop the skills and strategies they need to participate more fully during writing workshop.

Types of Mini-Lessons

There are four basic types of mini-lessons (Avery, 1993):

1. Procedures
2. Skills
3. Strategies writers use
4. Qualities of good writing

Procedural mini-lessons deal with the operation and management of your writing workshop. You may discuss management issues such as how to transition from whole-group to independent writing, how and where to store "works in progress," how to manage a writing portfolio, and so on. Mini-lessons involving skills are concerned with the conventions of English usage that are important to help readers gain meaning. Skill lessons include attention to punctuation, grammar, word usage, capitalization, and spelling. When teaching a "strategies writers use" mini-lesson, you will focus on techniques for writers that facilitate the writing process, such as selecting topics and planning a piece. Mini-lessons that help students to consider ways to improve their writing are categorized as "qualities of good writing" mini-lessons. In these mini-lessons, students learn about such writing techniques as using strong leads, writing an effective ending, elaborating, and using dialogue. We will go into greater detail about mini-lessons in chapters 2–7.

Characteristics of Effective Mini-Lessons

According to Avery (1993), effective mini-lessons have four essential features. First, they are short. While some will be lengthier, most effective mini-lessons are approximately 5 minutes long. Children need to spend the bulk of writing workshop engaged in writing, not listening to you. Second, mini-lessons are focused. Although there may be several issues that you need to address with your students, they should not all be emphasized in one day. With mini-lessons, "less is more." A brief focused lesson on one skill or strategy is more likely to be understood and applied than a longer lesson that addresses multiple topics.

The third quality of effective mini-lessons is that they are gentle in tone. Mini-lessons are not mandates, and you should not expect your students to return to their seats and immediately apply the new skill or strategy to their writings. Instead, we think of mini-lessons as invitations. The message is "Here is an idea that might make your writing more interesting. Why don't you play around with this idea sometime?" We're not implying that you adopt a laissez-faire attitude toward skill development. The remainder of this text will assist you in skill development, scaffolded instruction, and accountability issues.

The fourth characteristic of effective mini-lessons is that they are responsive. The content of your mini-lessons will be determined by the needs of the writers in your class. Certainly you'll need to utilize the skills and objectives outlined in your state and district curriculum guides. After developing your scope and sequence at the beginning of the year, you will remain flexible based on the needs of your students. You will examine your students' writings routinely to help you determine the skills and strategies that you want to address in an upcoming mini-lesson.

Guiding Children's Writing

As we've stated previously, utilizing children's literature, modeling in front of the students, and providing appropriate mini-lessons are powerful ways to guide students. We also work to guide students' writing by encouraging them to choose their topics; building a classroom community; instructing whole groups, small groups, and individuals to meet the needs of everyone; and allowing plenty of time for sharing.

The Importance of Choice

Choice is essential for writers to flourish. They must have ownership of an idea in order to be motivated to write well. Writers have two sources from which to choose topics: their experiences or their imagination. When teachers select the topic, the students no longer have these sources of information to enable them to develop a topic. We are not implying that "anything goes." For example, you may direct the students to write a nonfiction piece or a poem, but the topic (though not necessarily the format) is their own choice. We think you will find that this freedom of choice dramatically improves your students' writing and motivates them to become better writers.

We've seen teachers give their students story starters or prompts in a misguided attempt to help them select topics. While a few students may connect with the prompt and write eagerly, most students we've seen respond with contrived writing and an unenthusiastic manner. We recognize, however, that some states have mandated writing tests that require students to write to a prompt. If you are in a state with this requirement (as we are), this should be a small part of your total writing program.

Building a Community

The whole-class lessons that you initiate during writing workshop establish a shared understanding that helps to create a community of learners. As Bill Teale (1995) asserts, "I see building a sense of community as one of the most important things that we as language arts educators can do, both for ourselves and for our students. A feeling of belonging engenders responsibility, caring, and commitment" (p. 80). Writing workshop establishes shared common values, goals, and activities; builds social bonds; and allows students to blossom. Trust is established, it is safe to take risks, and mistakes are seen as opportunities for learning. Children become motivated and excited about reaching their potential as writers.

Meeting the Needs of Individuals

Besides the whole-group instruction you provide during writing workshop, you must also meet the needs of individuals. Not all students need the same things at the same time. For some students, your mini-lessons will be a review and a reinforcement of what they already know. For others, the lesson is just right, and they are ready to apply it in their own writing. For still others who are not quite ready to use the skill, your mini-lesson will be a preview. Careful assessment and small-group or individual instruction are also necessary for writing workshop to be successful. More information on developmental stages of writing, assessment, and small-group instruction can be found in chapter 8.

The Importance of Talk

For primary students, silence is the enemy of writing. Talking about their writing is crucial during writing workshop. Although you will need to establish expectations for acceptable volume levels, it is important to hear a hum of noise around your classroom. Sharing their ideas helps students to plan their writing by talking through their intentions. As they listen to others, students piggyback off a peer's writing to get ideas of their own. A student who reads a piece to a peer may find parts that need editing or revision. Primary students are reluctant to change their writing, but they often catch errors or omissions when they have the opportunity to read their pieces out loud. Sharing their writing with others also helps to promote the attitude that the class is a community of learners and writers. Students share their writing or listen to the writing of others, compliment or critique each other's work, and establish a camaraderie that supports writing development. Finally, sharing helps to honor each student's voice. It communicates that "Your words are important, and we all want to help and support you as a writer."

Other Opportunities for Writing

Writing workshop is a necessary but insufficient route for developing students' writing. Writing will occur throughout the day, not just during the half hour or so of writing workshop. Writing can easily be integrated into other content areas. When writing is integrated into reading, math, social studies, or science, students have authentic purposes for writing. Other writing opportunities that we've found useful with primary students include literature response, learning logs, treasure books, and literacy stations.

Literature Response

As we share literature with children, we want students first to listen and enjoy. To explore deeper meanings and observe students' comprehension, oral and written responses are appropriate. To improve students' responses, Taberski (2000) recommends that we provide more time for responses (both oral and written), help children to interact, and improve our questioning techniques. She cautions, however, that an unbalanced attention to written responses demotivates students and keeps them from reading. Taberski also recommends that we be careful about the frequency and types of literature responses we ask students to make.

   Taberski utilizes four types of written responses in her primary classroom: (a) writing about a favorite part, (b) relating the book to one's life, (c) summarizing what the book is about, and (d) relating the book to other books. Her basic rule is for emergent and early readers (generally in kindergarten and first grade) to respond in writing once every 2 weeks, and for transitional and fluent readers (usually in second grade) to respond weekly. This frequency guideline seems reasonable to us. It shouldn't burn out students on written responses or take away from reading time. Figure 1-2 shows an example of Jennifer's (a first grader) written response to *The Relatives Came* (Rylant, 1985). It says:

> This story reminds me about the time when my mom's cousin
> came to visit us. We got to go to a wedding. I was a flower
> girl. I slept with my mom so they could sleep. I liked to play
> with her girl. Her name was Megan. They came in June or
> July. We got to go to my cousin's birthday party. Her name was
> Megan. When it was time for them to go, I was sad but not
> too sad. We all said, "Goodbye!"

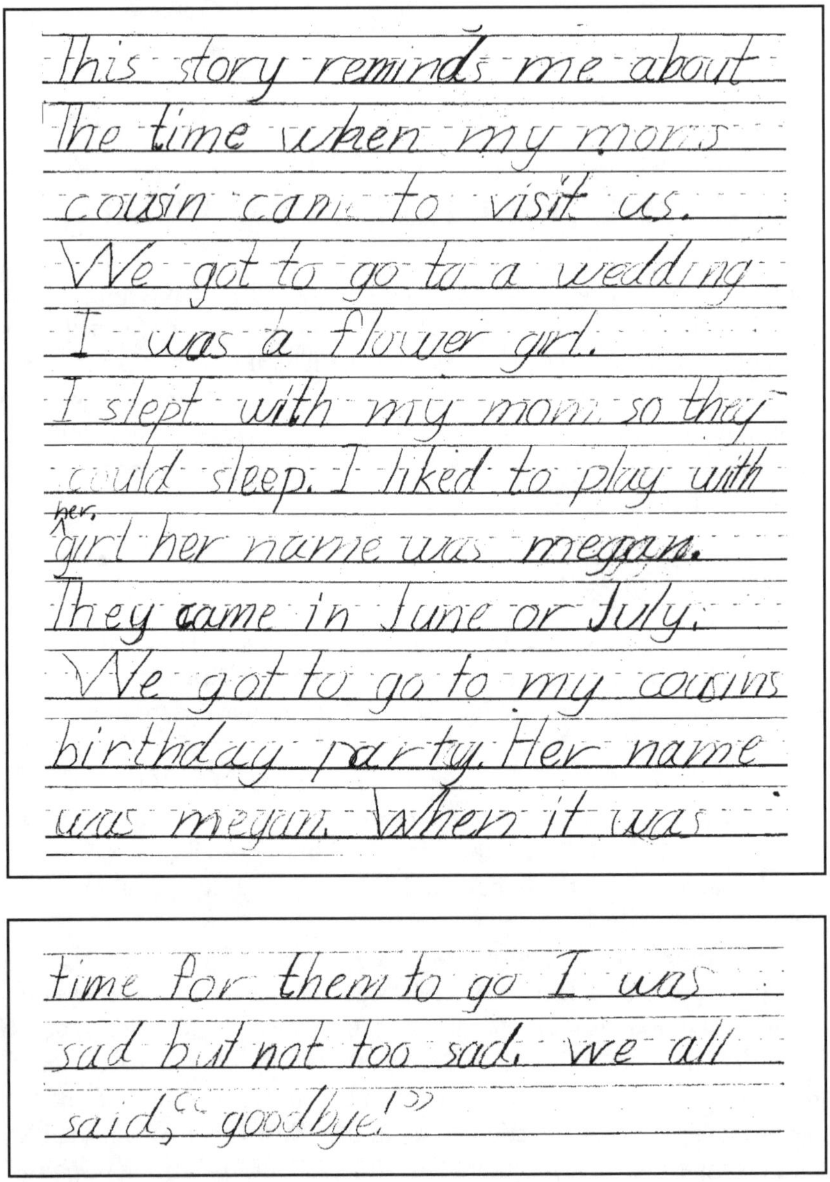

This story reminds me about
The time when my mom's
cousin came to visit us.
We got to go to a wedding
I was a flower girl.
I slept with my mom so they
could sleep. I liked to play with
her,
girl her name was megan.
They came in June or July.
We got to go to my cousins
birthday party. Her name
was megan. When it was

time for them to go I was
sad but not too sad. we all
said, "goodbye!"

Figure 1-2.   Example of Literature Response

Learning Logs

Routman (1991) defines a learning log as a vehicle in which "the student communicates how and what he has understood about a concept or unit of study.
Students describe their learning processes—that is, 'writing to learn'" (p. 229).
Learning logs provide opportunities for students to write about what they are
learning in social studies, science, math, art, physical education, or music. You
may ask the students to predict, analyze, connect, or reflect on their learning in
these content areas. Debbie has her students supply a spiral notebook for their
learning log. Any time that content writing is appropriate, students use this
notebook for their entries. Figure 1-3 shows a learning log entry from Shirl's
first-grade class. Marco wrote about his observations after an experiment with
water. The task was to use the materials (wax paper, toothpick, eyedropper, a
small cup of water, and a paper towel) to discover as much as possible about the
properties of water. It says: "Dragging the toothpick to the drop made it split

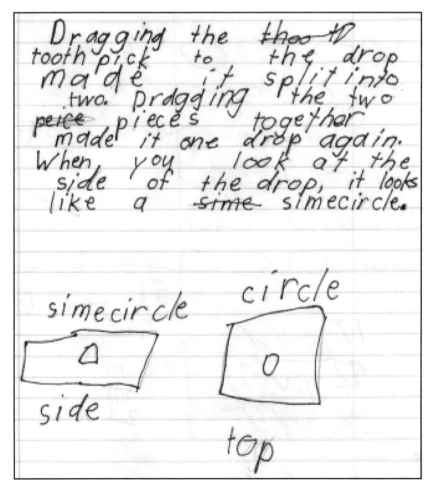

Figure 1-3.   Example of Learning Log Entry

into two. Dragging the two pieces together made it one drop again. When you look at the side of the drop, it looks like a semicircle."

Treasure Books

"This is how I write. I take a moment—an image, a memory, a phrase, an idea—and I hold it in my hands and declare it a treasure" (p. 8). After reading this statement by Lucy Calkins (1994), Shirl began using treasure books in her classroom. Treasure books are like a journal, in which students record memorable moments while they are also constructing longer pieces during writing workshop. Often these shorter images will trigger a memory that they can develop into a longer piece. Shirl tells the students that every moment of their lives is a treasure that is worthy of being recorded, and the treasure book is where they can write these events for future reminiscences. The students use black-and-white composition books, which are sturdy enough to last the entire year and chronicle each child's growth as a writer. (More information on Shirl's treasure books is found in chapter 5.)

A treasure book entry is shown in Figure 1-4. Tran could not speak, read, or write English at the beginning of the school year; this entry was written toward the end of the year. It says:

> At night, me and my sister and mom go to Kroger, and my sister buy'd me a fruit rollups. And it's a tattoo and you can stick the picture on your hand. And first you need to get little bit water and put it on your hand and count to five or ten.

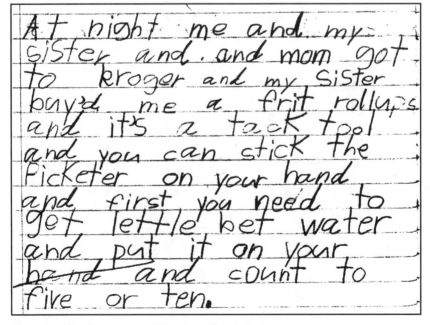

Figure 1-4. Example of Treasure Book Entry

Literacy Stations

Literacy stations (or centers) allow students to explore and practice literacy tasks while the teacher is working with a small group. Our literacy stations generally contain a writing component. In addition, we keep a writing station mainly as a supply center with a variety of paper, pencils, markers, tape, and so on. We encourage students to use these supplies throughout the day when they have an opportunity to record information. In this way, students see that writing is functional in various settings. Figure 1-5 shows a three-page sign that Randy (one of Shirl's students) made to protect his Lego block construction. The signs say: *Please do not touch!!!!!! If break, call Randy. If touch, Randy is very, very, very, very mad!*

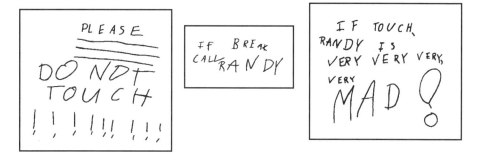

Figure 1-5. Signs at Literacy Station

Looking Forward

We've laid some groundwork for you in this chapter by relating the basics of raising young writers. The remainder of this book will be devoted to descriptions of our work in kindergarten, first grade, and second grade. We have tried to craft this book so that each chapter can stand solidly on its own, but all the chapters also work collectively to create a resource for primary teachers.

Our instructional practices change continually as we grow as literacy professionals. This is certainly not the final word on writing instruction for primary students, but we hope that you will glean some ideas for enriching and sustaining your writing program.

Chapter

2

Introducing
Writing Workshop

*We all learn by doing, reflecting on what we've
done, and improving our first attempts.*

—Donald Graves, *A Fresh Look at Writing*

One of Shirl's favorite pastimes is scrapbooking. She makes beautiful photo albums that demonstrate her careful attention to content and composition. When she first began this hobby, however, she was a total novice. Shirl had seen and enjoyed lovely scrapbooks made by others, but she lacked knowledge of their construction. To tackle her first scrapbook, Shirl took a class from a knowledgeable teacher. In this class, the teacher was the "master" scrapbooker and Shirl and the other students were the "apprentices." At first, Shirl and the others had limited knowledge of scrapbook construction and required explicit instruction, assistance, and encouragement from the teacher. Some students easily mastered the skills more quickly than others. With practice, persistence, and support, Shirl is now a master scrapbook maker herself.

We think that Shirl's scrapbooking experiences are a good metaphor for writing instruction. Just as Shirl initially needed explicit instruction, assistance, and support, your students will require the same elements as they begin writing.

You will serve as the master teacher while your students are the apprentices. Like Shirl's scrapbooking teacher, you will need important knowledge and skills to successfully implement writing workshop in your classroom.

You'll begin writing workshop during the first weeks of school. This chapter will describe how Shirl and Debbie initiate writing workshop in their first- and second-grade classrooms. We will describe the first 3 weeks or so, when we establish routines, procedures, and practices for our writing workshop program. We'll discuss selecting topics; planning our text to model our own writing process; matching pictures to words; adding details; using sound spelling and the word wall; and learning about conventions of books such as the title, dedication, copyright date, and publishing location. If you are a kindergarten teacher or have students functioning at the kindergarten level, we'll explain adaptations for these writers in chapter 5.

Initial Preparation

Before beginning your first day of writing workshop, you'll need to set up your classroom to facilitate writing workshop routines. You'll also prepare several items that will be used during the first week of instruction. Although you'll spend a little extra time preparing for writing instruction, this effort will pay off for you as your writing workshop routines become established.

Organizing the Classroom

We both have spaces in our classrooms where students can sit on the floor together for whole-group instruction. This close proximity to the teacher helps to establish a warm and intimate atmosphere. The closeness also helps to ensure that all students can view any books you read or texts you write. In addition, we have our students' seats grouped so that conversation among the students is easy during writing workshop. As long as you establish clear expectations about acceptable noise levels, your students will benefit from being able to talk with one another as they plan, write, and revise their work. We organize student desks in groups of four or five. You'll also want areas around the room to which students can move when they need a quiet spot to work or a place to sit with a partner for a writing conference. Figure 2-1 is an example of a classroom floor plan designed to facilitate writing workshop. We encourage you to adapt this plan so that it works best for you.

In addition, you'll need a place to store students' writings. One container will contain "works in progress." We don't let students keep their writing in their desks—their work can be lost or damaged there. Instead, each day we pass out the writing that they're working on and then collect it at the end of writing

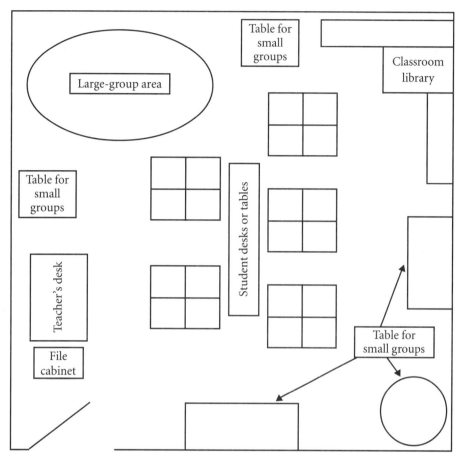

Figure 2-1. Classroom Layout

workshop. Students will also need a place to keep the writing that they've finished. Neither of us sends completed pieces home as the students finish them.
We like to keep their completed works and refer to them throughout the year.
It's fascinating to see the growth as the year progresses! After a joyous celebration, students take home all of their writing on the last day of school.

You'll probably want each student to have some kind of writing portfolio in
which to store their completed work (see chapter 8). Shirl stores completed
pieces in hanging files. In some years, Debbie also has used hanging file folders;
in others, she has had her students make their own portfolios by folding pieces
of poster board in half and stapling the sides. Regardless of the portfolio system
we've used, students have been encouraged to access these folders to review
their past work or to share their writings with their parents.

Establishing the Environment

The environment that you establish is essential for the success of your writing workshop. We hear teachers talk about making their classrooms risk-free. We strongly disagree with this characterization. Instead, we want our students to take risks, not just with writing but in all content areas. As students take risks with their writing, they expand their repertoire of writing skills and strategies, experiment with writing techniques, and work on finding their voice as a writer. Instead, we like the term *threat-free*. Your classroom environment remains supportive as you encourage students to take risks. In this threat-free atmosphere, mistakes are seen as opportunities to learn and improve.

Preparing for the First Week

Several items must be prepared before you can initiate writing workshop. You'll construct a writing folder and a five-page book (described below) for each child. In addition, you'll make a poster to record topic ideas that will be used during the second day of writing workshop (see Table 2-1). We'll tell you more about how to use these items later.

Table 2-1. Topics Chart

Authors Write About . . .	
Things They Have	People They Know
Places They Go	Things They Do

Writing Folders

The writing folder is used all year as a place for students to record topic ideas, titles of books they've written, and words they want to learn to spell. Figure 2-2 shows the contents of the writing folder; it's simply a three-pronged pocket folder. (Masters for the inside sheets of the writing folder are available in the appendixes or on our Web site.) We make double-sided copies (pages 1 and 2 on one sheet, pages 3 and 4 on another sheet) so that the spelling sheets are adjacent when the folder is open. The recording sheets are then hole-punched and placed in the pocket folder, one folder for each student. You'll make one for yourself, too. We'll explain how we use these later in this chapter.

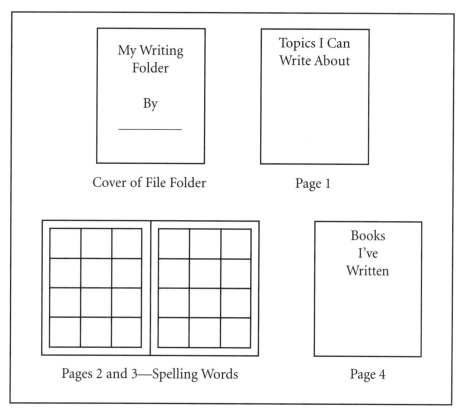

Figure 2-2.   Writing Folder Contents

Five-Page Books

"Five-page books" are the heart of our writing workshop. They are simply five pages of paper stapled into a construction paper cover. Writing on one topic, students compose and illustrate using this format. We use this format as a ve-hicle for helping children to understand story structure, leads, endings, elabo-ration and many other strategies writers use. Five-page books create a supportive structure for emerging and developing writers.

Students use the first page for the beginning of their writing, the next three pages for the middle of their piece, and the last page for the end of the writing. After attending a state literacy conference in which Mary Ellen Giacobbe shared her writing experiences, Shirl experimented with Giacobbe's ideas and began using this five-page format. She discovered that it facilitated the writing devel-opment of her first grade students. Debbie tried it with her second graders, and she also found that her students became better writers with the five-page book format. We'll discuss how we utilized the five-page book format in the next section.

As we've stated, five-page books are five pages of paper stapled into a sheet of construction paper. At the beginning of first grade, Shirl uses plain blank paper as her five pages. About midyear, she substitutes primary handwriting paper with lines in the bottom half. Debbie begins her second graders' year with the half-lined paper, but midyear she offers fully lined paper for students who do not want to illustrate their writing. (Lined paper templates are available in the appendixes or on our Web site.) Our covers are 12-by-18-inch sheets of construction paper, folded in half to make 12-by-9-inch folders. We choose light-colored paper so that students' book covers are easily visible. We usually make the first set of books one color, the next set another color, and so forth. This is advantageous because the teacher can easily determine which students are working on their first book, which students are working on their second, and so on. Some years, however, we've had very competitive classes in which students rush through a book to get to the "same color" as their friends. When this happens, we make all of our books with a white cover to alleviate this problem. Before introducing writing workshop, we prepare one class set of five-page books, including one for us to use as we write in front of the children.

The five-page book format has worked well for both of us, but we don't mean to imply that students may write only five pages. If students have a topic that requires more than five pages, they can easily remove the staples and insert extra sheets. Also, this format is not meant to be a structure in which students complete page 1 on Monday, page 2 on Tuesday, and so on. In the next section, you will see that five-page books allow for flexibility and encourage students to progress at a pace appropriate for their own development.

The First Few Weeks

As we describe the first few weeks of writing instruction, we'll take a look at Debbie's second-grade classroom as she introduces procedures and practices of writing workshop. We'll describe the intent of each lesson, show how Debbie teaches each mini-lesson, and share her written product after each day's lesson. In addition, we'll explain the students' tasks after each mini-lesson. Although we use Debbie's writing as our example, Shirl's lessons are comparable. You'll follow a similar format with the same objectives, but of course the topic you choose to write about will be different.

Throughout this book, we will recommend that you write in front of your class. As you do that, you'll "think out loud" so that children can gain a view into the thinking processes that proficient writers undergo. We'll give examples of our thought processes as we think aloud with our classes. In this chapter, we'll use Debbie's example as she modeled her first five-page book to her second graders at the beginning of the school year.

Lesson 1: Considering the Work of Authors

The intent of Debbie's first lesson is to help her students begin to think about what a writer does to compose a piece of writing. Students also learn about and decorate the writing folders that Debbie has prepared for them.

Mini-lesson. Debbie first reads aloud either *Author: A True Story* (Lester, 1997) or *What Do Authors Do?* (Christelow, 1995). Both books are good for helping young writers begin to consider the workings of authors. After a class discussion, Debbie briefly introduces the contents of the writing folder (see Fig. 2-2). She tells her students that they will learn how to use its contents over the next few weeks. Using her own writing folder, she models writing "My Writing Folder by Ms. Rickards" on the front, and then she decorates it with an illustration of her choice. After this, Debbie passes out a writing folder to each student.

Students' task. For this introductory day of writing workshop, the students have a simple task. Just as Debbie did, they write "My Writing Folder by ____" on the front of their folder and then decorate it as they wish.

Lesson 2: Learning About Authors and Their Ideas

This lesson focuses on where authors get their ideas. Debbie completes it over a day or two in her second-grade class. Shirl completes this activity with her first graders during the first 6 weeks before beginning the five-page book format. (See how Shirl adapts her beginning-of-year instruction in chapter 5.)

Mini-lesson. Debbie tells the students that most authors get ideas from their own lives. Using a stack of selected children's books, she gives a quick synopsis and tells where the authors got the ideas for each book (see Table 2-2). (It's an added bonus if some of these books have been read to the class prior to this lesson.) Debbie's intent is to help her students see that published authors get their ideas from incidents in their own lives and that her children can, too.

Table 2-2. Author's Ideas

Where Did The Authors Get Their Ideas?		
Title	Author	Idea
Twinnies	E. Bunting	The author wrote about her twin granddaughters.
Potato: A Tale From the Great Depression	K. Lied	The author wrote about something that happened to her own family.
Nana Upstairs, Nana Downstairs	T. DePaola	The author wrote about childhood memories of his grandmother and great-grandmother.
The Art Lesson	T. DePaola	The author wrote about his memories of first grade.
My Rotten Red-Headed Older Brother	P. Polacco	The author wrote about her childhood relationship with her brother.
Meteor	P. Polacco	The author wrote about something that happened to her family when she was a child.
Pink and Say	P. Polacco	The author wrote about a family story from the Civil War.
Thank You, Mr. Falker	P. Polacco	The author wrote about her fifth-grade teacher.
When I Was Young in the Mountains	C. Rylant	The author wrote about memories of her childhood in Appalachia.
Alexander and the Terrible, Horrible, No Good, Very Bad Day	J. Viorst	The author wrote about her son.
Snapshots From the Wedding	G. Soto	The author wrote this after he attended a wedding.
Grandfather's Journey	A. Say	The author wrote about his grandfather's life in Japan and his adventures in America.
My Great-Aunt Arizona	G. Houston	The author wrote about the impact that her great-aunt had on the lives of others.

Allowing time for talk. Next Debbie asks the students to think about any stories they might have in their own lives. She might ask for a few students to tell their stories in front of the class. Then she puts students in pairs so that they can discuss their pieces together. We like Marcia Freeman's (1998) idea of knee-to-knee discussions. The two students face each other with knees together to better facilitate their conversation. Debbie moves from group to group and listens to each discussion, prompting and complimenting as needed.

We strongly emphasize the importance of allowing students enough time to talk together. In young students, talk often functions as a form of planning and rehearsal. In addition, young writers also piggyback off of each other's ideas; thus, listening to others serves as a way to find new topics on which to write. Your writing workshop will never be silent. Productive talk is beneficial and will pay off by improving the quality of your students' writing.

After Debbie's students have had 5 minutes or so in their knee-to-knee discussions, students contribute ideas for the class topic chart (see Table 2-3 for a partially completed list). This list will be a class reference all year long. Students can use the list for getting topic ideas and for checking their spelling. Debbie ends this lesson by asking students to continue to think about other topics about which they might want to write.

Table 2-3. Topics List With Entries

Authors Write About . . .	
Things They Have • pets • families • toys	People They Know • parents • brother and sister • teacher
Places They Go • zoo • school • vacation	Things They Do • take a bath • cook dinner • wash the dog

Lesson 3: Considering Our Own Topics

During this lesson, Debbie and her students consider topics that they can write about, ensure that they have enough information about a particular topic to complete a five-page book, and begin the "Topics I Can Write About" list found in the writing folder.

Mini-lesson. Debbie first reviews the information that was discussed in Lesson 2—where authors get their ideas. She might read one of the titles from yesterday's lesson and further discuss the author's ideas. Then she models how students can consider ideas for their own topics lists.

For this lesson on creating a topics list (Figure 2-3), Debbie's think-aloud went something like this:

> Well, I want to write about things I know about, just like the authors we've talked about. I could write about teaching because I know a lot about that. I'll put "Teaching" on my topics list.
>
> You know I just had a new grandson born, and he came to visit me this weekend with his parents. I could write about Michael.
>
> I could write about video games. Let me make sure I have enough information. I know that kids play them, sometimes at home and sometimes at the mall or restaurants. I know . . . oh, I don't think I know enough information to write about that topic. But I do know a lot about a trip that I just took this weekend to San Antonio. I could write about that. I know a lot about my mom, and she might want to read a book that I've

> written about her. I also could write about something from when I was a kid. I bet you'd like to hear the story of when my sister hurt my favorite stuffed animal. His name was Beany Bear, and my sister was really mean.

After adding a few more topics, Debbie says, "That's all the topics I can think about now. But I can keep adding to my list whenever I think of something that I might want to write about."

Students' task. Just as in Lesson 2, students will first pair up for a knee-to-knee discussion. Debbie asks them to think about a couple things about which they'd like to write. They then orally rehearse their ideas, deciding if they have enough information to complete a five-page book. Debbie moves from group to group and supports their discussions. (Once the students actually begin writing, you may find that some students begin a book without having enough information for five pages. We'll deal with that issue in chapter 3.)

After allowing ample time for knee-to-knee discussions, students return to their seats and fill out several ideas on their "Topics I Can Write About" list in their writing folder.

TOPICS I CAN WRITE ABOUT
Teaching
My New Grandson
My Trip to San Antonio
My Mom
Beany Bear
Dan, the Chef
Our New Car
Kelsey

Figure 2-3.   Teacher's Topics List

Lesson 4: Introducing Five-Page Books; Beginning Page 1

During this lesson, Debbie first discusses how books have a beginning, a middle, and an end, and she introduces the concept of the five-page book. She also uses this lesson to establish several important precedents that she will use all year as she models her own thought processes as she writes. She chooses a topic, makes sure that she has enough information to complete five pages, plans her pages orally, and shows children how to deal with writing mechanics such as punctuation and spelling.

Mini-lesson. Debbie first reads and discusses a book with a clear beginning, middle, and end, like *The Mitten* by Jan Brett (1990). She uses five fingers as a visual representation of the five pages of the organization of this book. (Students also will use this technique in their own writing workshop books.) This visual aid will help students to better understand that they need enough information to write five pages on one topic. The lesson begins like this: "Now that we've read *The Mitten,* I want to show you how Jan Brett made sure she had enough information to write this book." Debbie holds up her hand to show five fingers. "She began the book with Nikki wanting a mitten, so his grandma knitted one for him." She holds up her thumb only. "Then he loses it." Debbie holds up her next finger. "Many animals fit into the mitten." She holds up her middle finger. "Finally the mitten bursts." She holds up her fourth finger. "The story ends when Nikki gets his mitten back." Debbie holds up her little finger.

Debbie introduces the five-page book during this lesson, telling students that they'll complete a book so that everything in the book is about the same topic, just as Jan Brett did. She again holds up her hand to show five fingers. She tells the students that they will all write a book with five pages. The first page will be their beginning. (Debbie holds up her thumb, and then shows students the first blank page in a five-page book.) The next three pages are for each student to write the middle of the piece. (Keeping her thumb up, Debbie holds up her middle fingers, and then shows the middle three pages.) Finally, she holds up her pinkie finger and tells the students that the last page of each book is for the ending.

Before beginning this lesson, Debbie had already selected a topic about which she wanted to write. She chose to write about one of the topics from her topics list—Beany Bear. Debbie has mentally rehearsed her piece so that she's prepared to model the writing in front of her class. She knows that she'll want to think out loud about her topic selection, its composition, and what to do when encountering a tricky spelling word.

The spelling strategies introduced in this lesson build on spelling lessons that we've already used with our students. We both utilize a *word wall,* which helps to teach high-frequency words and displays them for reference (Cunningham, 1991). We have previously modeled the stretching out of words so that we can write the sounds we hear in the word. Debbie tells her students that this is *turtle talk*—saying a word slowly, as a turtle would, to help us hear all the sounds. In chapter 5 we'll discuss other word work that we do.

Debbie's think-aloud continued like this:

> Yesterday you seemed interested in hearing more about the story of my mean sister and my Beany Bear, so I've decided to write that book for you. First, though, I need to make sure I have enough information for my five-page book.

Debbie holds up her five fingers as she thinks aloud.

> On the first page, I can tell about getting ready for a dance recital and how I got to wear a fancy costume. It made my sister jealous. I can write about her jealousy on page 2. Then, on page 3, I can tell how my sister went into my room and stole Beany Bear. Next I can tell what she did to Beany Bear. On the last page, I can tell how she got in trouble!

Debbie and her students agree that she has enough information for five pages. Debbie begins her first page. Figure 2-4 shows her text.

> I know I want to tell my reader that I was getting ready for my dance recital. I'll say, "When I was six years old, I got to be in a dance recital. I got to wear a fancy costume." Now I'm ready to write. I'll use the word wall to check the spelling of <u>when</u>. It's w-h-e-n. When I was . . . No, w-u-z isn't the way to spell <u>was</u>. It sounds that way, but I know it's w-a-s. I'll just draw a line through my mistake and keep writing. When I was six . . . I'm not sure how to spell <u>years</u>, so I'll write the sounds I hear if I turtle-talk the word. Y-e-r-s.

Debbie continues writing, demonstrating how to think about the message, consult the word wall, and sound-spell words of which she isn't sure. When she completes the writing, she begins the illustration.

> Now I'm ready to draw my picture. I know my picture has to match my words. I've told about getting dressed in my costume for my dance recital, so I think I'll draw me in my costume. It had a frilly collar, so I want to make sure I show that. I'm not a very good artist, but I'll do my best.

This last statement was made in order to head off comments by students such as "I don't know how to draw this." Our response to comments such as these has always been "I know you'll do your best." We also hope that these "amateur" illustrations will help to assure you that you don't have to be an artist to model illustrating a text for your students.

Giving spelling help. As students begin writing workshop, many students ask for help with spelling. We've found that students tend to rely on us exclusively if we function as their "spelling dictionary." We have two strategies to combat this tendency. Most often we say, "Use the sounds you hear and write those on your paper, or turtle-talk the word." This helps to make the students more independent and develops their phonemic awareness. Occasionally, if it is a high-frequency word that is not yet on the word wall, or if it's a word that the student will use

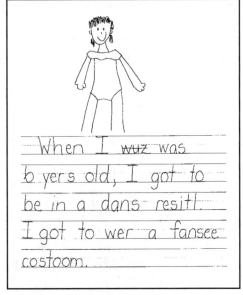

Figure 2-4.   Page 1

throughout the book, we write the word in the "Words I'm Learning to Spell" section of the student's writing folder.

Students' task. Students return to their seats and choose a topic. Debbie walks around and asks them to tell their topics and discuss their five pages. With individuals, she again models, using five fingers to visually represent their five ideas. If students finish selecting a topic that would complete a five-page book, they then begin page 1.

It is important to note that students will now begin to be at different points in the writing process. At the end of this lesson, some students will still be considering a topic. Others will have finalized a topic but will not have begun writing. Still others will be hard at work on their first page. You will want to pace your initial lessons so that students have only a brief time to work. While you are introducing writing workshop procedures, you want your writing to stay well ahead of the students'.

Lesson 5: Thoughtful Illustrations; Revising Page 1 and Writing Page 2

In this lesson, Debbie discusses how illustrators make thoughtful illustrations to help the reader understand and enjoy the text. This lesson also introduces the important concept of revision. Young students are often reluctant to revise, and revision for primary children is typically additive—they will add information but usually won't delete or rearrange text. With this lesson, Debbie wants to establish the habit of looking at our work and improving it each day. We call this *revisiting*. Every day she models revisiting what she wrote the day before and considering improvements to the text and illustrations.

Just as we used our five fingers, we now use another visual aid to signify revisiting. We first place our two hands with palms pressed flat together, then open them like a book and say, "We open our book . . ." Then we put our hands to our eyes like they are eyeglasses and say, ". . . and revisit our writing." This visual representation helps students to use revision habitually. When we find that students are reluctant to revise, we've learned that if we make colored pencils available, students eagerly select their favorite color to add or change their text or illustration. This also helps us to easily identify the revisions.

Mini-lesson. *The Art Lesson* (dePaola, 1989) is an excellent book for demonstrating the concept of thoughtful illustrations. In order that she has plenty of time for the rest of this mini-lesson, Debbie reads the book to the class beforehand (either a day before or earlier in the same day) so that the students are familiar with the story line. During this writing workshop mini-lesson, Debbie reviews the story and discusses the illustrations. She talks about the details in the pictures that Tomie dePaola used to help us enjoy the book and learn more about the text. Mary Ellen Giacobbe calls these pictures *thoughtful illustrations* because it is evident that the artist was thoughtfully considering the reader when he or she illustrated the book.

Debbie continues this lesson by teaching her students the visual representation for revision. Then she says the following:

> The first thing I want to do is revisit what I wrote yesterday. I'll reread what I wrote and see if I can make it better. "When I was six years old, I got to be in a dance recital. I got to wear a fancy costume." I like that, but I think my reader might be interested to know what my costume looked like. So I think I'll add, "It was red and had a special collar."

Debbie consults the word wall and uses sound-spelling to add this sentence at the end of page 1 (Figure 2-5).

And I think I could add some more details to my illustration. I wasn't standing there in the middle of nowhere! I was in my bedroom, so I'll add my bed with my stuffed teddy bear that I kept on it. There was a big window in my room, too, so I'll also add that.

I've finished revisiting my first page, so now I'll start on my second [Figure 2-6]. I've already told my readers that I was getting ready for my recital, so now it's time to tell them that my sister was jealous of me because no one was paying attention to her. I think I'll say, "My little sister was jealous. I was getting all the attention."

Figure 2-5. Page 1 Revision

As we've shown in past examples, Debbie uses the word wall and sound-spelling. "I'll draw my sister now. She was in diapers, and she had curly hair. I'll show her mad face." Debbie ends this lesson by reminding her students to revisit their writing and illustrations and to make sure that their pictures are thoughtful.

Students' task. After retrieving their five-page books, students return to their seats and first revisit their work from the day before. Then they begin wherever they left off. Some are still considering their topic, most are continuing with page 1, and a few are revising page 1 and beginning page 2. Debbie again paces her lesson so that students have only a little time to work, so that her writing stays ahead of the students'. As students begin to work, Debbie monitors to ensure that all students are rereading and considering revision of their text and illustrations.

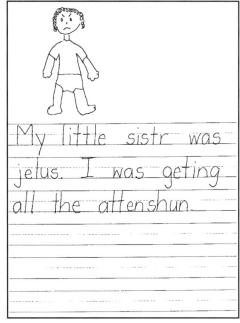

Figure 2-6. Page 2

Lesson 6: Learning That Pictures Match Words; Revising Page 2 and Writing Page 3

In this lesson, students will learn that their pictures must match their words. Debbie will model the revision of page 2, and then she will write her third page.

Mini-lesson. Debbie uses the book *George Shrinks* (Joyce, 1985) to help students see how pictures match the text. This is a short book that's easy to complete during this mini-lesson. As each page is read, Debbie and her students discuss how William Joyce made sure that the pictures correspond with the words.

Next, Debbie reviews her five-page plan so students will see that it is important to get in the habit of considering the "big picture" before revising the individual pages:

> Let me think about my plan. My first page was about my costume, and my second page was about my jealous sister. I want my third and fourth pages to tell what my sister did to Beany Bear, and my last page will tell how she got in trouble. Do I have enough information for five pages?

Debbie is now ready to revise the second page of her piece. She models the visual representation for revisiting. "First I need to revisit my work from yesterday. I open my book, and then I revisit." Debbie rereads page 2. "Oh, I notice I didn't tell my sister's name. I'll squeeze in *Laurie* right here" (Figure 2-7). Debbie writes her sister's name. She intentionally doesn't use a caret. "My picture shows that Laurie was mad, but I forgot to use words to tell my reader. I'll write, 'She got really mad!' I'll put one of these marks, called an *exclamation mark*, to show her strong feelings."

Figure 2-7. Page 2 Revision

Debbie continues:

> I need to add more details to my picture to make it a thoughtful illustration. Laurie was standing in the living room when she got so jealous, so I'll add the couch, a lamp, and some pictures on the wall. I think I'll also put in a speech bubble. I'll have Laurie say, "That's no fair!" I think now my reader will really find this page interesting.
>
> It's time now for me to begin my third page [Figure 2-8]. I remember that Laurie went into my bedroom, but I didn't know what she planned to do. I'll write, "She snuck into my bedroom to do something mean. She saw Beany Bear." Beany Bear was my favorite stuffed animal. I slept with him every night. I'll draw Beany Bear on my bed with Laurie sneaking into my bedroom. I want to make sure my pictures are thoughtful and that they match my words.

Figure 2-8. Page 3

Students' task. Again, students revisit their previous work and continue to revise and write. Debbie monitors her students' work to help them plan, revisit, write, sound-spell, and use the word wall.

Lesson 7: Adding Details With a Caret; Revising Page 3 and Writing Page 4

This mini-lesson introduces the use of the caret as one way to add information to the text. Any well-written children's book with many details could be used during this lesson. Debbie will also revise her third page and write her fourth.

Mini-lesson. Debbie selects the book *Sylvester and the Magic Pebble* (Steig, 1969) to establish the value of elaboration in writing. She decides to read only half of the book so that she can use the second half in Lesson 8 to introduce good endings. Before beginning the book, Debbie sets the purpose for listening.

> Remember when we talked about making thoughtful illustra-
> tions? We saw how adding details to our pictures helped the
> reader to better understand our ideas. Authors also add de-
> tails to their words. The author of this book does such a good
> job of using details. I want you to listen for all the details that
> William Steig wrote to help you understand the story.

As she reads, Debbie stops occasionally to discuss the details that the author
used.

When she finishes reading and discussing the first part of *Sylvester and the
Magic Pebble,* Debbie's instruction turns to her five-page book:

> I'll reread what I worked on yesterday because I know I need
> to revisit my work to see if I can make it better. I want to try
> something that writers use to add information. It's called a <u>caret</u>.
> It's not like a carrot that you eat!

Debbie shows the difference between the spelling of *caret* and *carrot.*

> The caret looks like a little arrow that points to what the writer
> wants to add. I think I'll say that Laurie was quiet when she
> came into my room because she was being sneaky, so I'll use
> the caret to add the word <u>quietly</u> [Figure 2-9]. I'll add that
> Laurie saw Beany Bear "on my bed" so the reader will know
> where she found him. I told you yesterday that Beany Bear
> was my favorite toy, but I forgot to write that for my reader. So
> I'll add the sentence, "He was my favorite toy." I see that I
> forgot to draw the window in my bedroom, so I'll add that,
> too.

Debbie continues:

> Now I'm ready to begin my
> fourth page. I want to tell what
> Laurie did to Beany Bear. It was
> terrible! I got to wear lipstick for
> my dance recital, and Laurie
> took that lipstick and smeared
> it all over Beany Bear! I'll write,
> "She took Beany Bear into my
> mom's room and got her lipstick.
> She put lipstick all over Beany
> Bear!" [Figure 2-10]. I think I'll
> just draw a big picture of Beany
> Bear. That will help my reader
> to easily see how bad he looked
> with the lipstick all over his face
> and body.

Figure 2-9.   Page 3 Revision

Students' task. The students retrieve their own five-page books and continue the writing process. As usual, Debbie moves throughout the room to monitor students as they address the skills she has taught. She provides support as needed to ensure student success.

Lesson 8: Writing a Good Ending; Revising Page 4 and Writing Page 5

This lesson focuses on the quality of good endings. Mini-lessons later in the year will concentrate more closely on this quality. In this lesson, Debbie wants her students to develop an ear for when a story sounds finished. She will also revise her fourth page and write her ending.

She took Beany Bear into my mom's room and got her lipstik. She put lipstick all over Beany Bear!

Figure 2-10. Page 4

Mini-lesson. To start with, Debbie reviews the first part of *Sylvester and the Magic Pebble* so the students recall the story line. Then she tells the class that because she'll be working on the ending of her Beany Bear story, she wants to finish *Sylvester and the Magic Pebble* to learn how William Steig wrote his ending. She directs the students to listen and determine when the story ends. As she reads the second half of the book, she stops occasionally and says, "The end!" Students then protest because they can hear that the story is not yet finished. When the read-aloud is complete, the class discusses how the author used his words to show the reader that the story had ended.

Next Debbie directs her attention to her five-page book. "I'm going to use the caret that we talked about yesterday to add some more information" (Figure 2-11). "I want to say that Beany Bear was sweet. I also will add a few more words." Debbie uses carets to add *bed, red,* and *poor.* She continues:

> Readers like to know about how the people in the story feel, so I'll also tell how angry I was when Laurie hurt Beany Bear. I'll write, "Now I was mad!" I really need to use that exclamation mark to show my strong feelings. I'm just going to change my picture a little bit.

I'm ready now to work on my ending page. I need to tell my readers how this story ended [Figure 2-12]. Well, of course I was upset, so I told my mom what Laurie did to Beany Bear. I'll write, "I went to tell my mom what Laurie had done. Laurie got in trouble and she never hurt him again." I'll draw a close-up of my mom and Laurie in the living room by the lamp. My picture shows that Laurie was sad because she got in trouble.

She took ∧ sweet Beany Bear into my mom's bed ∧ room and got her red ∧ lipstik. She put lipstick all over ∧ poor Beany Bear! Now I was mad!

Figure 2-11. Page 4 Revision

As Debbie writes, she uses the word wall and sound-spelling for tricky words.

Students' task. By now, the writing routine is becoming habitual. As we've said, Debbie wants her writing to stay ahead of her students during this initial five-page book. By this time, most of the students will be working on pages 2, 3, and 4 of their own five-page book. Debbie continues to monitor and support.

I went to tell my mom what Laurie had done. Laurie got in trubbl and she never hurt him again.

Figure 2-12. Page 5

Lesson 9: Revising Page 5 and Selecting a Title

This lesson helps students to consider good titles. Debbie introduces the "five-finger rule" when selecting a title. The rule specifies that titles can have five words or fewer. Five is an arbitrary number, but it helps prevent young writers from selecting titles that turn into a full summary of the book. We've found that our children will write titles such as *The Day I Went to the Park and My Mom Came and So Did My Dad*, or *My Dog Is a Cute Dog and I Like to Play With Him and I Love Him*. The five-finger rule helps to eliminate this problem.

To prepare for this lesson, we select several children's books that we think have good titles, such as *The Very Hungry Caterpillar* (Carle, 1969), *Night Noises* (Fox, 1989), and *The Amazing Bone* (Steig, 1976). With one of the books, we cover up the title. (You can buy special glue—we've seen products called re-movable glue stick, removable adhesive, or removable poster tape—that works like the glue used on stick-on notes. This glue adheres to a piece of paper to cover the title, and it is easily removed.) Debbie also has 3-by-3-inch stick-on notes available for this lesson.

Mini-lesson. Debbie first revises the ending to her five-page book (Figure 2-13):

> It's time for me to revisit my ending. I think I want to show that I didn't just walk into the living room to tattle on Laurie, I <u>ran</u> to my mom. I'll draw a line through <u>went</u> and put <u>ran</u> instead. I'll add the words <u>mean</u> and <u>bad</u> with carets so that it says <u>mean Laurie</u> and <u>bad trouble</u>. I think it's kind of confusing where I wrote, "Laurie never hurt him again." I will change the word <u>him</u> to <u>Beany Bear</u>. That way my readers will know that I'm talking about Beany Bear staying safe from Laurie. I can add some details to my illustration, too. I'll add the couch that's next to the lamp in the living room. I'll also make a picture of myself in the background. I'll draw a happy face, since I want to show that I'm glad Laurie's getting in trouble!

Figure 2-13. Page 5 Revision

Next Debbie turns to the children's books she has selected for this lesson. As she shows the books to the class (not yet showing the book with the covered title), she introduces the five-finger rule for selecting a title. (Some titles, such as *Alexander and the Terrible, Horrible, No Good, Very Bad Day* [Viorst, 1972], obviously have more than five words. If this comes up, we tell the class that occasionally an author will decide on a long title, but not usually.) Debbie and her students discuss how titles help us to know the subject of the book. Then Debbie shows the book with the covered title. She gives a brief synopsis of the book and asks the students to suggest titles that might fit the book. Finally, she uncovers the title, and the class discusses the author's title choice.

After that, Debbie thinks aloud about titles she could choose for her five-page book.

> Now I need to decide on a title for my book. I know I want to follow the five-finger rule, and I want my readers to know something about my book from the title. I could call the book <u>My Costume</u> or <u>My Mean Sister</u>. Those both follow the five-finger rule. What about <u>My Sister Hurts My Favorite Toy</u>? No, that has six words. I think I'll choose the title <u>Beany Bear</u> because I think my readers would be interested in a book about a stuffed animal. I won't put my title on my cover yet because I want to plan my illustration first. I'll just write the title on this stick-on note so I don't forget.

Debbie puts the stick-on note onto the cover of her book and then passes out five-page books to the students.

Students' task. Students continue the writing routine. If any students are ready to consider a title, Debbie directs them to write the title they've selected on a stick-on note. Then she suggests that they revisit the pages of their five-page book to see if they can add more details that would help the reader understand the piece better.

Lesson 10: Planning and Illustrating the Cover

In this lesson, Debbie helps her students to understand that cover illustrations are designed specifically to attract a reader's attention. In addition, she teaches them about the different layouts they can consider for their cover illustration.

To prepare for this mini-lesson, Debbie again selects one children's book with an attractive cover picture and an interesting layout. Using the removable glue stick and a piece of blank paper, she again covers the title but leaves the illustration showing. She also picks one book with no illustration. (Some hardback books have a plain cover once the jacket is removed.) In addition, she collects a stack of books that have interesting and colorful layouts.

Mini-lesson. To begin this lesson, Debbie holds up the illustrated book with the hidden title and asks the students to guess what the book is about, using the cover picture to help them. After removing the paper covering the title, she leads them in determining that the title and the illustration are related. Next Debbie holds up both books—one with an attractive cover and one with no illustration. She asks, "Which book would you rather read?" The students are naturally drawn to the book with the illustration. The class then discusses the function of the cover illustration. Debbie says the following:

> Because I want my readers to be attracted to my book, I want my cover to be beautiful. So I know I need to think carefully about my illustration. I could draw a picture of Laurie scribbling lipstick all over Beany Bear. However, I want the problem to be a surprise to my reader, so I don't want the cover to show Beany Bear after he got messed up. Maybe I could draw Laurie getting in trouble. Or maybe I could just draw Beany Bear on the cover. That illustration would match my title.

Looking again at the stack of children's books, Debbie and her students next study different layouts for the title and cover illustration. They observe that the title is sometimes at the top, sometimes at the bottom, and sometimes in the middle. Sometimes the title is part of the illustration, and other times it's separate. They also notice that some of the illustrations give many details, and some give just a few. Debbie continues, "I think I'll put my title at the top of my cover page and my illustration in the middle. I'll make the letters real big to attract my reader's attention." Debbie writes *Beany Bear* near the top of the cover (Figure 2-14). "I think Beany Bear would look good inside a big circle." She draws the illustration in the middle. "Now I need to let my readers know who wrote this book, so I'll write my name at the bottom."

Students' task. The students continue their writing. Most students will be working on the fourth or fifth page of their five-page book, but some students will still be working near the beginning. That's okay, as long as all students have been staying on task. Debbie continues to monitor and support her young writers.

Lesson 11: Writing a Dedication

The function of this lesson is to introduce the purpose of an author's dedication. Before beginning this lesson, Debbie gathers several books that include dedications. She has also prepared the following sentence strip:

> This book is dedicated to
>
> _____ .

Figure 2-14. Cover

Mini-lesson. Debbie begins as follows:

> Today we're going to learn about dedications. When authors write books, they often dedicate the book to someone special in their lives. The dedication lets the person know that the author was thinking of him or her while writing the book. Let me show you a couple dedications.

Debbie shares some of the dedications in the books that she's gathered.

> Now I need to dedicate my Beany Bear book to someone that's special in my life. My mom is special to me, so I could dedicate this book to her. My class is special, so I could dedicate it to you, but since this book is about my sister Laurie, I think I'll dedicate it to her. I'll just copy the dedication sentence off of the sentence strip that I have here.

She copies the sentence onto the back of the front cover. Later she will display the sentence in the classroom so the students can copy it as they write their own dedications. (Instead of writing the whole dedication sentence, Shirl's first graders just write, "To _____.")

Students' task. As usual, the students retrieve their own five-page books and continue the writing process. Debbie moves throughout the room to monitor students as they address the skills she has taught. She provides support as needed to ensure student success.

Lesson 12: Including Copyright Date and Publishing Location

This lesson teaches about copyright dates and publishing locations. Prior to this lesson, Debbie gathers several books with various publication dates. It's nice to have a book published long ago, such as *Millions of Cats* (Gag, 1928). Debbie has also prepared the following:

> ©200__
>
> Houston, Texas

Mini-lesson. Debbie begins, "All books have information about when and where they were published." She shows several books and tells the students the year each book was published. She also reads all the cities in which the publishing company is located. Sometimes Debbie and her students use tally marks to determine how many years have elapsed since each book was published. She continues, "I want to include this information in my book, too. I'll copy this at the bottom of the front cover" (Figure 2-15). Just as with the dedication sentence, Debbie displays this throughout the school year.

Students' task. The writing workshop routine continues. Some students are probably nearing the end of this first five-page book. As Debbie assesses her students' progress with their books, she determines if some students are almost ready to begin their second book. If so, she prepares another set of five-page books, changing the color of the cover on this new set.

This book is dedicated to my sister Laurie.

© 2001
Houston, TX

Figure 2-15. Dedication

Lesson 13: Telling About the Author

Though not always included in children's books, information about the author is usually found on the book jacket of a hardback book. This lesson introduces students to the "About the Author" section of their five-page book, which will be placed on the inside back cover. Debbie first finds several books that have a section that tells about the author.

Mini-lesson. Debbie begins, "Wouldn't you like to know a little bit about the authors of some of the books we've read? Well, the books I'll show you today all have a section called 'About the Author.' Let me read some to you." She reads the information from the books she's selected. "I need to have an 'About the Author' section in my book about Beany Bear. I could tell lots of things about me, but in this book I think I'll tell a little bit about my sister and me." On the inside back cover, Debbie writes her information, as shown in Figure 2-16.

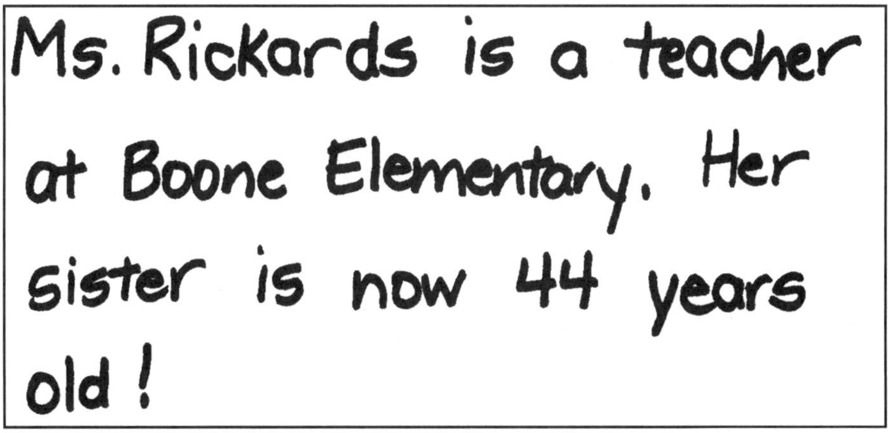

Ms. Rickards is a teacher at Boone Elementary. Her sister is now 44 years old!

Figure 2-16. About the Author

One option. Included in some "About the Author" sections are photographs of the author. Often we will either photocopy pictures of our students or use a digital camera so that they have the option of including a photograph in their five-page book. After seeing the photograph of Eve Bunting as a child in the "About the Author" section of her book *Twinnies* (Bunting, 1997), Debbie included the photograph of herself and her sister in her *Beany Bear* book (Figure 2-17).

Figure 2-17. Author Photo

Students' task. The writing workshop routine continues. Most students are finishing the text of their five-page books.

Lesson 14: Numbering the Book and Recording in the Writing Folder

To complete the first five-page book, the final task is to number the text and record the title in the writing folder.

Mini-lesson. First, Debbie holds up her writing folder and reminds students of the three sections: topic ideas, spelling words, and finished book titles. She turns to the "Books I've Written" section in her writing folder and says,

> Now that I'm finished with the book, I want to record the title in my writing folder. Because this is my first book, I'll put a small "1" in the corner of the cover of <u>Beany Bear</u>. Then I'll record the title and today's date in my writing folder [Figure 2-18]. When you finish a book, you'll record the date and title in your writing folder and then share with a friend. After that, you'll come to me for a conference.

Students' task. Students continue to work on their first five-page book. They are all at different stages of completion. Debbie monitors, supports, and reteaches as needed.

An Example

Figures 2-19 to 2-25 show an example of Linda's initial attempts at writing a five-page book. Debbie modeled the process of introducing writing workshop for Linda's teacher in February, so this example was taken from the second semester of first grade. Linda's book is entitled *My Family* and says the following:

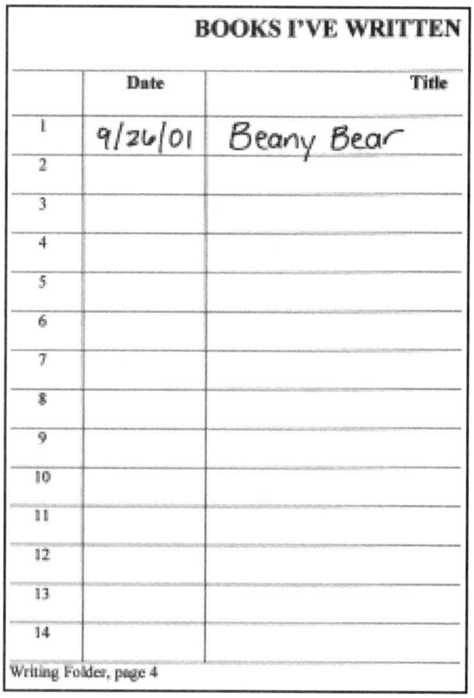

	Date	Title
BOOKS I'VE WRITTEN		
1	9/26/01	Beany Bear
2		
3		
4		
5		
6		
7		
8		
9		
10		
11		
12		
13		
14		

Writing Folder, page 4

Figure 2-18. "Books I've Written" Page

[Page 1] My family is very nice. I gave a rabbit to my nice sister, and my sister gave me something back. My sister likes to play with me lots more, but she doesn't take turns.

[Page 2] I like them so much. My family and me play some games together. And we eat sometimes, and we play together. And sometimes we make our dad a sandwich.

[Page 3] Me and my sisters and my family do a very lot of things together. I like my family. I like playing with my family.

[Page 4] Me and my sisters and dad ride our bikes together. We know how to ride on no training wheels. And we go where cars go, too. We like each other.

[Page 5] I like my family because they are nice. And cook nice, too.

[About the Author] Linda is six years old. Linda has two sisters. Linda is a twin. Linda is in first grade.

Figure 2-19. Linda's Cover

Figure 2-20. Page 1

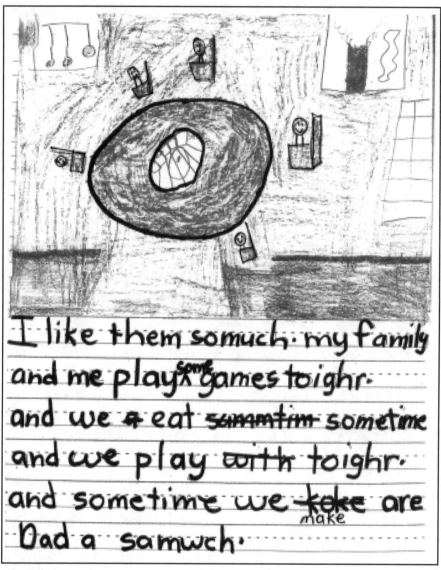

I like them somuch. my family
and me plays some games toighr.
and we ∂ eat summtim sometime
and we play with toighr.
and sometime we keke make are
Dad a samwch.

Figure 2-21.   Page 2

Figure 2-22. Page 3

Figure 2-23.　Page 4

I like my family becase thay are nice And coce nice to.

Figure 2-24. Page 5

Linda is six years old.
Linda has two sisters.
Linda is a twin.
Linda is in first grad.

Figure 2-25. About the Author

For a first attempt at a five-page book, Linda's piece has several strengths. She has stayed on topic, ensured that her pictures match the words, revised, and used sound-spelling. Although much more work is needed in subsequent books, Linda has clearly shown that she has understood and used the lessons that Debbie has taught. It's important to note here that Debbie is not expecting Linda to go back and correct all the errors. Although she'll continually model revision and editing throughout the school year, Debbie keeps in mind that her central task is to improve the writer, not the writing. Debbie has helped Linda to see many of the necessary elements of composing a good five-page book. When Linda is composing her next piece, she can use what she has learned from subsequent mini-lessons to improve her writing. Although we expect published pieces to be error free (see chapter 3), our day-by-day five-page books aren't.

What Comes Next?

At this stage of writing workshop, we've finished our introductory lessons. In writing workshop, because we are continually modeling our writing, we'll soon begin a new book of our own. As students finish their books, they first consult a chart posted in the room listing the following introductory elements to make sure they have all the necessary parts to their book:

- ✓ 5 or more pages
- ✓ Author's name
- ✓ Title
- ✓ Dedication
- ✓ Copyright date
- ✓ Publishing location
- ✓ About the Author

Next they share their book with a classmate, who checks for each element and gives feedback (see chapter 7). Finally, they'll come to us for a conference. We talk with them about their topic, give compliments, and discuss one or two goals for the next book. (This isn't the only conference we have with them; we talk with each student throughout the writing process [chapter 7]). We like to place a sticker, as shown in Figure 2-26, on the back of the book. We either make this sticker with our computer's label-making program or buy them commercially through a company that sells personalized address labels. This sticker signals to our students that they are finished with one book and ready to begin another.

Rickards Publishing Company
Second Grade
Boone Elementary
Houston, Texas

Figure 2-26. Publishing Label

Chapter

3

Target Skills

*We've learned that, right from the start, teachers need to teach **more**.*

—Donald Graves, *A Fresh Look at Writing*

Debbie's husband, Dan, is a pastry chef. When he was a student taking baking classes, the tools were unfamiliar and awkward. Eventually Dan learned the appropriate circumstances in which to use particular baking and decorating tools, and he became confident that he was using his tools in effective ways. Now Dan's use of his "tools of the trade" is automatic—the tools have become an extension of his craft.

Filling the Toolbox

Similarly, target skills are tools for our young writers. Target skills are the skills and strategies that writers use to write well—skills such as organizing, composing, elaborating, and revising. It's our job as teachers to instruct students about effective ways and appropriate places to use writing skills and strategies by "fill-ing their toolbox" with writing lessons. After reading *Teaching the Youngest Writ-ers: A Practical Guide* by Marcia Freeman (1998), we both began paying more attention to the importance of modeling and using direct instruction in these target skills and strategies. We considered what needed to be in each child's writing "toolbox" so that he or she could become a better writer. Having a list of target skills is helpful and necessary. However, the power of our lessons lies in their application. Therefore, we all must work to ensure that students use the tools in their toolboxes so that skills and strategies are used as an extension of the craft of writing, just as Dan's baking tools became an indispensable part of his pastry chef work.

We will begin this chapter discussing some general information related to the acquisition of writing skills and strategies—the "tools of the trade" for young writers. Then we will move on to more specifics by sharing a few ideas for mini-lessons, discussing an activity we call *target practice,* and sharing several plan-ning maps to help you prepare for instruction.

Consult an Expert

When we began writing this book, we consulted several other professional texts to see how published educational writers approached the writing task. We ad-mired Ralph Fletcher's voice clearly shining through in *What a Writer Needs* (1993) and *A Writer's Notebook* (1996). We studied how co-authors blended their voices in *Strategies That Work* (Harvey & Goudvis, 2000) and *A Teacher's Guide to Standardized Reading Tests* (Calkins, Montgomery, & Santman, 1998). We researched chapter length, format, titles, the balance between research and practice, and other concepts to help us make decisions about the kind of text we wanted to write.

We consulted these experts to help us become more thoughtful writers. By the same token, teachers can help students to become more thoughtful writers by en-abling them to see how published authors can teach them about different aspects of a writer's craft. Ralph Fletcher (1993) calls books that are used as examples of qual-ity writing *mentor texts.* Each children's book under study becomes a mentor to the students as they study a particular example of a writer's craft.

At her school, Debbie has designed a program called Consult an Expert. Debbie acquired a collection of children's books by writing several small grants. On each book, she has placed a label with the writing skill the book represents. As teachers plan for upcoming writing instruction, they use the Consult an Ex-pert books to prepare mini-lessons.

Now as we read children's books, we search for good examples of writer's craft. Anderson (2000) suggests several other sources for Consult an Expert ideas. He suggests that we involve students in the hunt for examples of quality writing. We can also use the student's own writing and excerpts from longer published pieces, or we can write a text ourselves to use as a mentor text. We're continually finding new sources that provide excellent examples to use with our young writers. The appendixes have a short list of titles, but our Web site has an extensive list of potential texts that you can use for your own Consult an Expert program.

You'll notice that most of our mini-lessons described in this book contain a literature component. We want to help our students learn "to take their own important topics and then look to texts to learn *how* to write well about those topics" (Ray, 1999, p. 10). We have one caution, however. Unless the Consult an Expert piece is very short, we don't read it during our writing workshop mini-lesson. Writing time is too precious to be used for a read-aloud opportunity. Instead, we make sure that we schedule time to read the Consult an Expert book prior to our use of the text as a writing tool.

Deep, Not Wide

Some target skills can be taught and mastered quickly. It's easy for children to understand onomatopoeia, for example. Still other skills, particularly those dealing with a writer's craft strategy like characterization or description, require a great deal of time and emphasis for students to use the skill well. For those skills, it's important that we cover them deeply and thoroughly. We don't want to cover too many skills quickly in order to pack more into our instruction; this makes the learning shallow, and the skill isn't likely to be solidly learned. As Zemelman, Daniels, and Hyde (1993) assert, "complete 'coverage' . . . results in superficial and unengaging teaching, like painting a room—plenty of square feet, but only one thousandth of an inch thick" (p. 123). Instead, taking time to delve deeply into a few important skills results in more in-depth understanding of a writer's craft. We try to keep in mind the phrase "deep, not wide" to remind us that it's our job to consider the target skills, analyze our students' skill levels, and pace our instruction to meet the needs of the young writers.

Target Skills

Throughout this book, we try to give you very explicit information about how we teach particular writing skills and strategies. Many of our lessons are described thoroughly in other chapters of this book. No text, however, can supply you with every writing lesson you'll ever need to teach to your young learners. Instead, what we hope to do in this section is to describe how we use graphics to teach target skills and to give you a few more ideas for mini-lessons.

Graphics for Target Skills

In chapter 2 you saw how Debbie introduced many writing skills during the first 3 weeks of writing workshop. To make the skills more visible, Debbie uses a poster with a large target and an arrow that reveal the day's target skill (Figures 3-1 and 3-2). When a new target skill is introduced, Debbie writes the skill on an arrow and then adheres the arrow so that it points to the bull's-eye on the target. When another skill is introduced, the arrow from the previous lesson is moved from the bull's-eye and replaced with the new arrow. The collection of arrows with all the skills previously taught becomes available for routine review on a separate chart.

Figure 3-1. The Writing Target

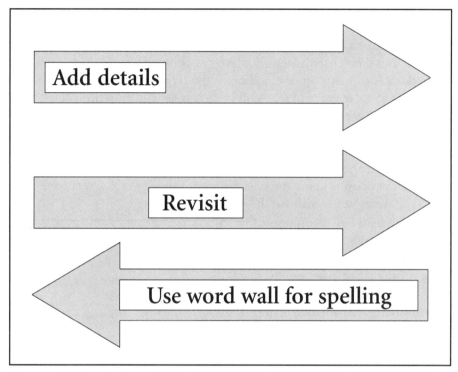

Figure 3-2. Sample Target Skills

Target Practice and Did-It Dots

Shirl successfully used target skills in her first-grade classroom—first, considering which skills to teach based upon her assessment of the needs of her young writers; second, designing her instruction to teach the skills; and third, supporting the use of the skills in the students' five-page books. Although she was pleased when a student applied the skills she taught, she was still dissatisfied because there were too few students using each target skill effectively. In response to this concern, Shirl designed the activity of *target practice.* After implementing this activity, she saw an impressive improvement in her students' use of target skills during their daily writing workshop.

Debbie also noticed that some of her young writers needed additional motivation to apply target skills during daily writing activities. She began using did-it dots after reading about the idea in Freeman's book (1998) on primary writing and, like Shirl, saw significant progress in students' use of target skills.

Target Practice

Target practice is a quick exercise in which students practice using a target skill isolated from their current work in a five-page book. Shirl uses target practice to check each student's understanding of the target skill; she's not expecting students to show mastery of that skill in their independent writing. First Shirl introduces a target skill, shares numerous examples from literature, and models its use. Then she gives the students a half-sheet of paper and invites them to practice applying the target skill. For example, after Shirl introduced the skill of onomatopoeia, she wrote a sample sentence and then asked each student to write a sentence using onomatopoeia. Figure 3-3 shows Fern's target practice. It says, "The skates went swish swash."

Once students have completed the assigned target practice, they turn it in to Shirl and then resume work on their five-page books. Shirl does a quick assessment to see who may need further help applying the target skill. She then identifies a small group of students who need more support, she reteaches the skill, and the group writes a sample sentence together.

Figure 3-3. Sample Target Skills

Shirl reproduces a form for each student entitled 'I've Hit the Target!' (Table 3-1). The form (available in the appendixes or on our Web site) is placed in each student's writing folder. Once a student has successfully completed target practice, Shirl encourages him or her to record the target skill on this form.

Table 3-1. Target Skill Recording Sheet

I've Hit the Target!	
Date	Target Skill

Did-It Dots

Did-it dots (Freeman, 1998) offer another way to reinforce students' use of target skills. The dots are round colored labels from an office supply store. The dots are placed on a student's writing when the teacher observes that he or she has applied a target skill. When we use a did-it dot, we write a code letter or symbol that signifies the target skill. Some sample codes are shown in Table 3-2. We also put a dot and a symbol onto the target skill arrow (Figure 3-4) so it can serve as a review and reference. Because a parent misunderstood the did-it dots, Shirl now writes a note home explaining their use so families don't think the did-it dot code is the child's grade!

As we walk around the classroom while students are writing, we observe each student's application of target skills. We carry our round labels and can quickly place did-it dots on many papers. In Figure 3-5, we show one page in Albert's five-page book. Albert is a first grader, and he has written, "I have a sister. She is almost 1 year old. She liked to play and walk. She does not like to get to sleep. She likes to eat a lot of food and drink a lot." As

Table 3-2. Sample Codes for Did-It Dots

Target Skill	Code
Add details	De
Revisit	R
Use the word wall	WW
Sound-spell	SS
Use alliteration	Al
Use Dialogue	" "
Use a thesaurus	T
Ask questions	?

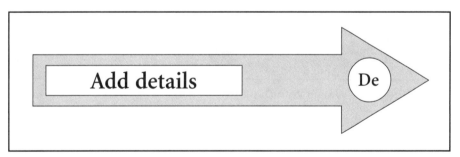

Figure 3-4. Target Skill With Did-It Dot

Albert worked on this page, he received a did-it dot for revisiting his previous writing (R), adding details to his illustration (D), and using sounds to spell the word *drink* (SS).

We've distributed did-it dots in various ways, but we always have them available daily. Sometimes we walk around the class, observe students who are applying that day's target skill, and award did-it dots. Other times we choose a skill learned previously and check every child's writing for that skill's application. Sometimes we visit students who haven't recently earned a did-it dot and search their writing for an opportunity to award one in any previously taught target skill. In addition, when we hold writing conferences (more on that topic in chapter 7), we give several did-it dots to celebrate skills used effectively.

Figure 3-5. Writing With Did-It Dots

More Mini-Lesson Ideas

Our mini-lesson ideas are embedded throughout this text. You'll find many ideas for writing lessons in chapter 2 (introducing writing workshop), chapter 4 (ideas related to writer's craft), chapter 5 (writing conventions), chapter 6 (nonfiction), and chapter 7 (responding). In this section, we'll offer a few more mini-lesson ideas that we've found helpful.

Revision by Rearranging Pages

One mini-lesson that we teach early in the process is how to use a staple remover so that pages can be rearranged if necessary. We've found several scenarios in which this is useful. Sometimes students simply need to change the order of the pages. Removing the staples from their five-page books allows them to reorder easily. Other times students will include pages that aren't related to their selected topic. In this instance, the student uses the staple remover to take out the pages that don't belong. These pages then go into the student's writing folder because they may be used for a topic that the child can expand on in another five-page book. Finally, students may need to add pages if they need more than five pages to finish a piece. We always model these forms of revision with our own writing to validate their use.

Revision With Spider Legs

A *spider leg* is simply an extra piece of writing paper that's taped onto the side of a page in a student's five-page book. The spider leg contains information that a student wants to add to improve his or her piece of writing. We first heard about spider legs from Mary Ellen Giacobbe at an early literacy conference in Dallas in November 2001. She calls them spider legs because they stick out to the side like a spider's leg. When we modeled this idea for our students, many became more motivated to revise. They liked the idea of adding spider legs to their writing! All that's needed to successfully implement spider legs is to have small strips of paper and tape available to the students.

Publishing

"Publishing (bringing a piece of writing to finished form) for real reasons and actual audiences motivates students to do their best writing" (Routman, 2000, p. 322). We can't, however, expect all of our students' writing to be polished enough so that it becomes part of our class library—the effort would soon overwhelm both our students and us. Instead, two or three times a year we help them to choose a five-page book for "publication." We require that students complete five or more five-page books before taking a text to publication. When someone is ready to publish a piece, we first confer with the student to discuss additional revisions. Then we (or a parent volunteer) type the student's writing, correcting errors just as a real-life editor would do for a published author. We give the student a choice of cutting out his illustrations from his five-page book and gluing them onto the published piece or redoing the illustrations for the published piece. Usually students want to redo the illustrations and improve on their first efforts. They understand that other students will enjoy reading their best work. We collect our class-made texts in a special basket, which becomes part of our classroom library.

K–2 Planning Maps

A planning map for writing serves several purposes. First, it allows you to plan the writing instruction for the students in your classroom. It helps you look at skills your students have already mastered and skills that need to be introduced and supported. Second, a planning map facilitates the delivery of a coherent and thoughtful writing program across grade levels. If your school uses a planning map for writing, you will know the skills that your students have already been exposed to in previous grades, what you are responsible for teaching while your students are in your class, and what the teachers in the next grades will teach. We provide three K–2 planning maps here as only one possible option of a scope and sequence for primary writing instruction.

Levels of Support

The planning map includes three levels of support: modeled, supported, and independent (see Figure 3-6). With some skills, you will just model; your intent is only to expose students to these skills. For example, you wouldn't expect kindergartners to write using quotation marks, but you might use quotation marks in some of the pieces you model for your kindergarten students. With other skills, you'll want your students to use them in their writing, but they will need some support as they experiment. Still other skills should be mastered, and you will expect your students to apply these skills independently. Each of these levels of support is used in a different instructional format.

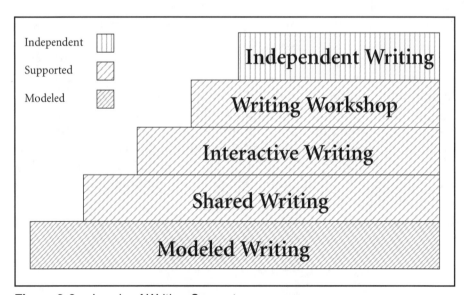

Figure 3-6.   Levels of Writing Support

In a modeled writing format, the teacher gives full support by modeling the writing process and thinking aloud. Modeled writing is what Debbie used in chapter 2 as she was writing her *Beany Bear* book in front of the classroom. During modeled writing, the students are observers only. Most often, modeled writing occurs during the writing workshop mini-lesson.

Supported writing occurs as students are composing the text and the teacher is providing various degrees of moderate support. Shared writing provides the most support. In shared writing, the students compose the piece (either in a large or small group) and the teacher acts as scribe. Interactive writing occurs when the students and teacher share the writing; this format is sometimes called *shared pen*. The students write as much as they can and the teacher fills in the rest. An interactive writing sample is shown in Figure 3-7. In this sample the students composed most of the text and the teacher supported them by writing the parts that are underlined. Writing workshop provides the least amount of support. The teacher supports students individually and through large- and small-group instruction.

Independent writing is a format in which students write independently with no teacher support. You will see students writing independently in their journals, in treasure books, in learning logs, or at literacy stations.

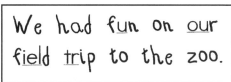

Figure 3-7.   Interactive Writing Sample

The Planning Maps

Tables 3-3, 3-4, and 3-5 illustrate planning maps that identify target skills for, respectively, the writing process, writer's craft, and written mechanics. We've delineated the skills by grade level, identifying which skills should be only modeled by the teacher, which skills should be used by the students with teacher support, and which skills should be mastered and practiced independently by the end of the year. We'll use one skill as an example: "Revisits and adds details to text with caret" in Planning Map 1. The map indicates that the skill should be modeled in kindergarten, supported in first grade, and independent in second grade. Instructionally, this means that kindergarten teachers would model the skill of adding details with a caret during modeled and shared writing. First-grade teachers would both model the skill and support students as they add details to their writing by using a caret. Second-grade teachers would model and support the use of this skill in a variety of writing formats, but they would expect second graders to independently use a caret to add information by the end of the school year.

Table 3-3.   Planning Map 1: Target Skills for Writing Process

	K	1st	2nd
Selects a topic	S	S	I
Makes picture match words	S	I	
Dictates message	I		
Writes labels, notes, and captions	M	I	
Plans writing orally	S	S	I
Revisits and adds details to illustration	M	S	I
Revisits and adds details to text with caret	M	S	I
Revisits and replaces words with better words		M	S
Reads in Author's Chair with appropriate volume	S	I	
When in Author's Chair, sets purpose for listening	M	S	I
Shares writing with partner	S	I	
When responding to writing, summarizes classmate's piece	M	S	I
When responding to writing, makes connections to classmate's piece	S	I	
When responding to writing, compliments classmate's piece	S	I	
When responding to writing, asks questions about classmate's piece	M	S	I
After the author has set a purpose for listening, makes an appropriate comment	M	S	S
Identifies relevant questions for inquiry	M	S	I
Takes simple notes from relevant sources	M	S	I
Compiles notes into a written report	M	S	I
Uses prewriting techniques such as drawing and listing thoughts	M	S	I
Brings selected pieces to publication		S	S
Reviews a collection of own work to monitor for growth	S	S	I
Edits for appropriate grammar, spelling, punctuation, and features of polished writings	M	S	S
Uses resources to find the correct spellings, synonyms, and replacement words	M	S	I

M = Modeled; S = Supported; I = Independent

Table 3-4. Planning Map 2: Target Skills for Writing Craft

	K	1st	2nd
Writes an interesting lead	M	S	S
Writes an interesting ending	M	S	S
Uses interesting words	M	S	S
Uses strong verbs	M	S	S
Tells what is happening or what happened	I		
Writes what is happening or what happened	S	I	I
Uses specificity	M	S	S
Uses color, number, size, and material words	M	S	I
Uses onomatopoeia	M	I	
Uses interjections	M	I	
Uses dialogue	M	S	S
Uses alliteration		M	S
Makes comparisons with simile, metaphor, and/or personification		M	S
Uses expanded sentences	M	S	S
Narrows a topic	M	S	S
Experiments with different genres	M	S	S
Writes a caption	M	I	
Writes a labeled diagram	M	I	
Writes a table of contents, index, and/or glossary		S	S
Identifies effective features of a piece using criteria generated by the class or teacher		M	S

M = Modeled; S = Supported; I = Independent

Table 3-5.   Planning Map 3: Target Skills for Written Conventions

	K	1st	2nd
Writes name on paper	I		
Uses appropriate spacing	S	I	
Writes left to right and top to bottom	I		
Wraps text to next line	S	I	
Recognizes the difference between words and letters	I		
Recognizes the difference between capital and lowercase letters	S	I	
Writes using mostly lowercase letters	M	I	
Uses a capital letter at the beginning of a sentence	M	I	
Uses a capital letter for a proper noun	M	S	I
Uses a capital letter for the word *I*	M	I	
Uses a period appropriately at the end of a sentence	M	I	
Uses punctuation (comma or exclamation point) after interjection	M	S	I
Uses a period in abbreviations		S	I
Uses a question mark appropriately at the end of a sentence	M	I	
Uses an exclamation point appropriately	M	I	
Uses quotation marks with dialogue	M	S	I
Uses a comma correctly when writing dialogue	M	S	S
Uses the word wall to correctly spell high-frequency words	M	S	S
Uses letter sounds and word parts to spell unknown words	M	S	S
Uses apostrophe to denote possession		M	S

M = Modeled; S = Supported; I = Independent

Our informal assessments help us to determine the length of time to devote to a particular target skill (see chapter 8). When we choose a writing objective to teach, we initially spend several days or more working with the skill. We use literature models, daily oral language activities, target practice, and sentence dictation (described in chapter 5) to reinforce each skill. We remind our students to check their written work to see if they've used a particular skill, and we expect them to edit their work if they haven't used the target skill. After we've modeled and supported the skill, we examine students' writing. We then re-teach the skill as needed. Thus our focus on a particular target skill is cyclical; we return to it occasionally throughout the school year.

We encourage you to study our suggestions in these planning maps and then revise them to meet your needs. We recommend that you work with your colleagues to arrange a scope and sequence that is best for your school, considering your state's and district's writing expectations.

Chapter

Moving Beyond
Competence to Excellence

*If our teaching is to be an art, we must remember that it is
not the number of good ideas that turns our work into an
art, but the selection, balance, and design of those ideas.*

—Lucy Calkins, *The Art of Teaching Writing*

When he was in middle school, Shirl's son liked to play computer games. As he became more competent, Josh utilized word processing programs in high school to complete his schoolwork. His knowledge level continued to increase. Today, Josh has a growing business that designs Web sites for his customers. We now phone Josh when we're stumped by the mysteries of technology. Josh has moved from competence with computers to excellence as he uses technology for business and pleasure.

As we used five-page books and target skills with our young writers, we felt like we were competent writing teachers. Our students were learning writing skills and strategies and loving writing workshop. But to move our teaching skills from competence to excellence, we needed something more.

In the fall of 2000, we both attended the Texas State Reading Association conference in Dallas. One of the presentations we heard deepened our practice in the use of target skills. The presenters, Kathy Stuart and Paula Groberg, shared an instructional idea that used the acronym DIMPLES to help intermediate students focus on the qualities of good writing. After experimenting with their ideas, we revised and reorganized the target skills for use with primary students. In this chapter, we'll describe how we use the acronym VOICES to extend our writing instruction. This format is recommended for use after you have other elements of writing workshop—five-page books, sharing, assessment, and small-group instruction—firmly understood and practiced. In fact, you may want to skip this chapter until you are comfortable with all the other essential elements described in this book. When you're ready, you'll see that by using the VOICES framework, your writing instruction will move from competence to excellence.

VOICES as an Organizational Tool

Introduction

VOICES stands for the elements of a writer's craft that we've found useful in teaching young writers (Table 4-1). V signifies vivid word choice; O means onomatopoeia; I stands for interesting dialogue; C is for comparisons; E indicates expansion of one idea; and S represents specificity. Within each letter category are several skills that we explicitly teach.

Table 4-1.   VOICES Framework

	Stands for . . .	Target Skills Included	Sample Sentences
V	Vivid Word Choice	Strong verbs, leads, and endings	The frog leaped over the log.
O	Onomatopoeia	Onomatopoeia and alliteration	Splash! The duck dives deep into the pond.
I	Interesting Dialogue	Interesting dialogue and interjections	"Wow! Look at that bug," said Tom. Billy replied, "It's a big cricket."
C	Comparisons	Similes, metaphors, and personification	The rain played a sad song on my head. My hair felt like a wet mop.
E	Expand One Idea	Expand one idea, narrow the topic, use transition words, and evoke emotions	Suddenly, a door creaked open. Out slithered an enormous dragon.
S	Specificity	Descriptive words and proper nouns	Rover found two big bones under the wooden table.

We first spend time teaching the skills of vivid word choice. Then, while periodically reviewing elements previously studied, we move on to the skills under O, then I, and so on. For each letter category, we use an illustrative icon and sample sentence. Each skill within the six categories has a rhyming couplet to help define the skill and to assist students in remembering the craft element. We also use nursery rhymes, popular poetry, and literature connections to help students identify and practice the target skills under VOICES. (One of our favorite poetry anthologies is *The Random House Book of Poetry for Children*, with poems selected by Jack Prelutsky [1983].) In addition, we devote a large bulletin board to VOICES, where we display the letter, icon, sample sentence, rhyming couplets, and assorted samples from literature and from students' writing (Figure 4-1).

Figure 4-1. VOICES Bulletin Board

We follow these lessons in the sequence presented in our VOICES framework, though presenting them in any order would be fine. We recommend that first-grade teachers devote approximately 1 month per letter, and second-grade teachers spend 1–2 weeks on each letter as a review. If your second-grade students are unfamiliar with the VOICES format, however, 1 month per letter would be appropriate. Kindergarten teachers can use the VOICES framework, too. One letter per 6 weeks would be about right for kindergartners, but we recommend that kindergarten teachers utilize only the literature component of these lessons. Kindergartners are unlikely to be developmentally ready to integrate the VOICES lessons into their own writing. We do VOICES lessons once or twice a week; the other days are devoted to mini-lessons designed in response to student needs, as determined by our routine assessment.

Preparation

Before you are ready to introduce each letter and its components, you'll need to prepare several graphics to use with each lesson. We find that reproducing these graphics on card stock and then laminating them increases durability. For each letter, you'll need posters of the letter, broad skill, icon, sample sentence, and rhyming couplets, all printed on 8 ½-by-11-inch paper. For many lessons, you'll also need nursery rhymes reproduced on chart paper or a transparency. You'll learn more about these components as we describe our lessons. Figure 4-2 illustrates the graphics necessary for introducing strong verbs (a subset of vivid word choice).

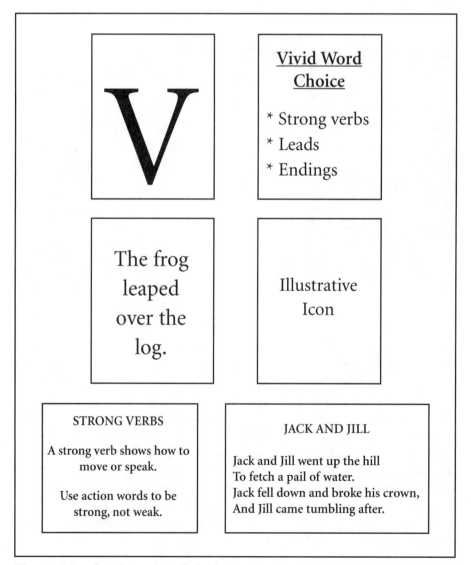

Figure 4-2. Graphics of a VOICES Lesson

VOICES Lessons

Our VOICES mini-lessons introduce each skill using a rhyming couplet, followed by discussion, modeling, and guided practice. Many of the lessons have a target practice component. As students find and create samples of each skill, they post them on the VOICES bulletin board. After each mini-lesson, students continue work in their five-page books. We encourage our students to use the VOICES skills in their own books, and we reward with did-it dots as we see students independently using each VOICES skill. As we've done before, we'll use examples from Shirl's classroom to explain the routines involved in teaching with VOICES.

V = Vivid Word Choice

As we introduce the category of vivid word choice, we include the target skills of strong verbs, good leads, and appealing endings. We use the sentence "The frog leaped over the log" as a sample sentence for vivid words. We also use a picture of a frog jumping over a log as an accompanying illustration. (You can, of course, make up your own sample sentence with a corresponding picture for this and all the examples presented in this chapter.)

Strong Verbs

The skill of strong verbs is introduced and practiced for 1–2 weeks. Several introductory mini-lessons are necessary first, and then you and your students practice identifying strong verbs until you think that most students have understood the concept and are ready to move on.

Lesson 1 begins with Shirl holding up the 8½-by-11-inch poster of the V. She says, "Today we are going to learn about something good writers do to make their pieces better. It's called *vivid word choice,* which means using words that give readers a good picture in their heads." She continues, "The V stands for vivid word choice." She shows students the sample sentence and says, "Here's a sentence that uses vivid word choice or exciting words. Let's read it together." After reading, Shirl asks, "What picture came into your head when you heard those words?" Students respond, and then Shirl displays the picture icon. "Here is a picture to remind us to use vivid or exciting words. It's just like the picture you saw in your head." Shirl leads the students in observing that *leaped* is a good word choice because it gives the reader specific information and helps the reader to visualize the author's meaning.

Shirl's lesson continues:

> When we listen to stories and poems over the next few days, we're going to be detectives searching for interesting action words. Action words are called verbs, so we'll be looking for words that give us a strong picture of the action. We'll call them strong verbs. When we find them, we'll write them on this chart.

Shirl introduces the rhyming couplet (Figure 4-3) and teaches the kinesthetic movement corresponding to strong verbs—students make a V with two fingers when they hear a strong verb. She says:

> I have a little poem that will help you to remember about strong verbs. When you hear a strong verb, you can think of the poem and hold up your fingers in a V to show that you're a good word detective.

Shirl then reads a short book, and the students listen for vivid verbs. If they hear one, they hold up the V sign. After the story is complete, they add the strong words they heard to the chart. If her students don't hear a strong verb in the selection, Shirl says, "I heard a strong verb on this page. Listen when I read it again and put up a V sign when you hear it." We recommend that you do this verb search in moderation. You don't want to interrupt every page of the story!

STRONG VERBS

A strong verb shows how to move or speak.
Use action words to be strong, not weak.

Figure 4-3. Rhyming Couplet for Strong Verbs

Lesson 2 begins with a review of the target skill and accompanying sample sentence, icon, and rhyming couplet. Shirl then continues the lesson by stating, "Today we're going to practice our target skill by using the nursery rhyme *Jack and Jill*." Shirl and her students read the poem that's been written on chart paper. She then says:

> When someone wrote this nursery rhyme, they used the word went to show how Jack and Jill moved up the hill. That's not a very strong verb! It doesn't tell us exactly how they moved up the hill. Did they march? Did they crawl? Did they skip? Let's see if we can think of other words that would give us a better picture of how Jack and Jill went up the hill.

As students offer suggestions, the class recites the first line of *Jack and Jill,* substituting a strong verb for *went.* As each suggestion is read, Shirl and her students act out the suggested movement.

Shirl spends another day or two working with other nursery rhymes as the children substitute strong verbs for the verb in the rhyme. Suggestions include *The Bear Went Over the Mountain* (changing the verb *went*) and *Jack Be Nimble* (changing *jumped* in the phrase "Jack jumped over the candlestick").

In the third mini-lesson, students practice the target skill by writing a sentence with a strong verb. First they review the sample sentence, icon, and rhyming couplet. Shirl continues, "Today we're going to do our target practice. We're each going to write a sentence that has a strong verb. We want to make sure that we use a word that makes a clear picture in our readers' minds." Shirl writes the sentence "I went down the street" to model how to give the reader a better picture. "In this sentence, I used the word *went.* Does that tell my reader how I moved as I went down the street? What's a word that would be better?" Shirl then crosses out *went* and writes a new choice. She asks, "What other words would make sense and give the reader a better picture?" After a discussion, Shirl says:

> Now it's your turn to try to hit the target! You can use my frame sentence, "I ____ down the street," or you can make up a sentence of your own and use a strong verb. After you write a sentence, you illustrate it. Bring it to me when you're finished, and then begin working on your five-page book. You might find a place in your five-page book where you can use a strong verb.

Shirl passes out paper for the target practice, and the students return to their seats to write a sentence including a strong verb. (An example of this target practice is shown in Figure 4-4. It says, "I zoomed to the park.") As children turn in their target practice, Shirl quickly checks the work and helps students who are struggling with the target skill. To close the lesson, Shirl asks several students to read their target-practice sentence to the class, and then they chant the rhyming couplet. Finally, Shirl says, "Tomorrow during writing workshop, when you feel your pencil writing a boring verb like *went* or *go,* think about switching to a strong verb to tell your reader *how* to move."

Shirl's next mini-lesson focuses on substitutions for *said.* The format of this lesson is similar to the lesson using *Jack and Jill.* For this lesson, Shirl and her students first review the rhyming couplet for strong verbs. She then introduces

Figure 4-4. Strong Verbs Target Practice

the rhyme *Five Little Monkeys Jumping on the Bed.* After reading the rhyme, students consider substitutions for the word *said* in the line "The doctor said, 'No more monkeys jumping on the bed.'" They repeat the line using alternative words with corresponding voice (e.g., *whispered, bellowed, shouted, screamed*), and Shirl writes them on stick-on notes (see Figure 4-5).

Figure 4-5.   Substitutions for *Said*

The next day Shirl and her students review the previous day's lesson, and then they practice the target skill on their own. Shirl models with the sentence "Mom said, 'Go to bed.'" She tells the students that they can either use her frame sentence, "Mom ____, 'Go to bed,' or they can write a sentence of their own, using a strong verb as a replacement for *said.* Student sentences should include who is talking (e.g., mom, dad, teacher, friend), what they are saying (e.g., go to bed, clean up, put your head down), and how they are saying it (e.g., with a scream, whisper, or cry).

Accomplished writers practice moderation in their use of strong verbs. Moderation is a difficult concept for first and second graders to understand, so you will want to be careful how you model and support the use of this skill. We try to encourage students to use one strong verb per page by thinking about which action they really want to make distinctive. If there are too many strong verbs in a piece, the writing sounds artificial and unnatural.

As these lessons are occurring, Shirl and her first graders begin collecting examples of strong verbs to display on the VOICES bulletin board. Shirl contributes cartoons that she has cut out of the newspaper. She staples a few target-practice sentences to the display. If students find a good example of a strong verb, they recopy it and contribute it to the display, too (as shown in Fig. 4-1). When children independently add a strong verb to their writing, Shirl places a did-it dot labeled with a V on their paper. Collections such as these become routine for each component of the VOICES lessons.

Leads

In this lesson sequence, Shirl introduces the meaning and purpose of a lead, teaches students one way to make a good lead, and assists students as they experiment with various leads for the pieces on which they are working.

The first mini-lesson begins with Shirl saying the following:

> When I watch a movie, I can usually tell right away if I'm going to like it. The beginning of the movie needs to be interesting and get my attention. Our writing is the same way. The beginning needs to be interesting and get our reader's attention. The first few sentences are called the <u>lead</u>. The lead hooks our reader into reading more.

Shirl introduces the rhyming couplet (Figure 4-6), and she and the students chant the rhyme several times. She continues, "One way that we can hook our reader with our lead is to show action. We learned all about action sentences when we talked about strong verbs." The class repeats the rhyming couplet for strong verbs and reviews a few of the sentences on the VOICES bulletin board under "Vivid Word Choice."

LEADS

A good lead is like a hook.
It makes your reader take a look.

Figure 4-6. Rhyming Couplet for Leads

Next, Shirl holds up *Alexander and the Terrible, Horrible, No Good, Very Bad Day* (Viorst, 1972). She says:

> We've read this book before. Alexander was having a terrible day! When Judith Viorst wrote this book, she wrote a lead that uses action. Listen to all the action words that she uses in the first page of this book. "I went to sleep with gum in my mouth and now there's gum in my hair and when I got out of bed this morning I tripped on the skateboard and by mistake I dropped my sweater in the sink while the water was running and I could tell it was going to be a terrible, horrible, no good, very bad day." Doesn't that lead hook you and make you want to read more? Let's chant our rhyme again.

When they are finished chanting, Shirl tells them to continue working on their five-page books.

For the second mini-lesson on leads, Shirl displays the nursery rhyme *The Three Little Kittens.* She reads the first line dramatically in a sobbing voice:

> "Three little kittens have lost their mittens and they began to cry." That lead makes me feel like I'm right there with those sad kittens. It makes me wonder what will happen next to these poor kittens. This nursery rhyme is an example of a piece that uses action as the lead. The action makes me want to keep reading.

Now Shirl is ready to model writing a lead of her own. She says:

> In this five-page book, I'm going to write about my dog Shiloh. I want to tell how Shiloh felt when my other dog, Lester, died. I could begin with "Shiloh was sad when Lester died." That's kind of boring, though, and probably won't hook my reader. I'll try to rewrite my lead to show action. How does this sound? "Shiloh searched everywhere for Lester and then howled a sad goodbye." I think those actions will make my readers curious and want to read more. When good writers begin a piece, they try to write a lead that will be interesting and get their readers' attention. When you are beginning a new piece, you'll want to think about using action to hook your reader.

The class chants the rhyming couplet for leads again before they continue working on their five-page books.

The third mini-lesson is used for target practice. Prior to the lesson, Shirl has written the nursery rhyme *Little Bo Beep* on a chart paper or transparency. After the class has said the rhyming couplet for leads and reviewed the previous day's work, she says:

> Today for target practice, we're going to use the nursery rhyme Little Bo Peep. We're going to experiment with different leads that show action. When we experiment, we try something in a different way. When writers do this, it's called revision. They try their writing in a different way. We're going to experiment with the lead for Little Bo Peep.

Shirl reads the nursery rhyme and then focuses on the beginning line, "Little Bo Peep has lost her sheep." She continues:

> We know that Little Bo Peep has lost her sheep, but we don't know why she lost them. If we were to experiment with a different lead, we could show what she was doing when the sheep got lost. Maybe we could say, "Little Bo Peep was picking flowers, and then she lost her sheep." Or we could say, "Little Bo Peep was reading a book, and then she lost her sheep." What are some other actions that Little Bo Peep could be doing when the sheep got lost?

As students suggest actions, Shirl writes them on chart paper, which will later be displayed on the VOICES board. After the students have brainstormed some possible actions of Little Bo Peep, Shirl gives them their target practice assignment. "Your job for target practice is to write a new lead that shows Little Bo Peep and her action. You might want to start your sentence with 'Little Bo Peep ___, and then she lost her sheep.'" Shirl writes this phrase on the board and distributes paper for target practice. When students have finished, they return to their five-page book. For students who struggled with the target practice, Shirl holds a small-group conference and they write a new lead together.

The fourth mini-lesson on leads focuses on the students' current pieces. Shirl asks the students to bring the five-page book they're currently working on as they gather on the floor. The class reviews the purpose for a lead and chants the rhyming couplet. Then she says, "Today we're going to look at some of your leads and see if we can experiment to make the lead show action. Who would like to start?"

Freddie volunteers and reads his lead: "I like to go roller blading." As two or three students offer suggestions for different leads showing action, Shirl writes their ideas on stick-on notes and gives them to Freddie. After several other students have read their original lead and received suggestions for other options, Shirl closes the mini-lesson by reminding the students that good writers experiment with their writing and often try more than one lead. (Shirl is not expecting Freddie or the other students to go back and use the stick-on notes to revise their leads, however. She keeps in mind that her job is to improve the writer, not the writing. Shirl is giving her students a strategy for improving their leads in future pieces.)

Shirl repeats this lesson a few times with other students' leads. She will revisit the topic of leads at several points later in the VOICES sequence of lessons, introducing the following types of leads:

✓ Onomatopoeia

✓ Alliteration

✓ Dialogue

✓ Interjection

✓ Comparison

Endings

To introduce students to appealing endings, Shirl first discusses boring endings. She says:

> Raise your hand if you like to be bored. Of course you don't!
> Readers don't like to be bored, either, but sometimes writers
> write endings that are boring. If a writer writes, "And then I
> went home" or "And then I went to bed," those endings make

> me bored. Sometimes writers end with "And it was all a dream." Endings like that make me think that the writer didn't know much about writing appealing endings. <u>Appealing</u> means interesting. Let's read our rhyme about endings.

After the class has chanted the rhyming couplet (Figure 4-7), Shirl continues:

> Our rhyme tells us three ways to write an appealing ending. When a story ends with a surprise, that's certainly not boring! So a good ending might end with a surprise to the reader. Sometimes authors write a <u>circle story</u>. In a circle story, the end circles back and is connected to the beginning. Sometimes writers end their pieces by using feelings. The characters in the story might feel happy or sad. Or the reader might have strong feelings at the end. The end might make the reader feel happy or sad.

Next Shirl displays three books that she has previously read to the class. Each

---

ENDINGS

**To write a good ending that's more appealing,
Use a big surprise, a circle, or a feeling.**

Figure 4-7.   Rhyming Couplet for Endings

book represents one of the three kinds of endings: surprise, circle, and feeling. In this example, Shirl uses *Flossie and the Fox* (McKissack, 1986), *If You Give a Mouse a Cookie* (Numeroff, 1985), and *Thank You, Mr. Falker* (Polacco, 1998). Shirl says:

> We've read these three books before. When we read <u>Flossie and the Fox</u>, we were surprised when Flossie tricked the fox. <u>Flossie and the Fox</u> is an example of a book with a surprise ending. <u>If You Give a Mouse a Cookie</u> has a circle ending. In the beginning, the mouse wanted a glass of milk, and at the end the mouse wants another glass of milk. The story circles back to the beginning. In <u>Thank You, Mr. Falker</u>, Patricia Polacco writes an ending that makes us have strong feelings. At the end of this story, we feel really good that Patricia has learned to read. Let's start a chart and write the titles of the books we read and the kinds of endings that they have.

Shirl writes the titles of these books on the chart (Table 4-2). (This chart will continue to be used throughout the year as the class reads other books and identifies the kind of endings they have. It becomes part of the VOICES bulletin board.) Students chant the rhyming couplet for endings and then continue work on their five-page books.

Table 4-2. Endings Chart

Surprise	Circle	Feeling
• *Flossie and the Fox*	• *If You Give a Mouse a Cookie*	• *Thank You, Mr. Falker*

Prior to the next mini-lesson, Shirl revises the nursery rhyme *Little Miss Muffet* and writes it on chart paper as follows:

Little Miss Muffet

Little Miss Muffet sat on a tuffet
Eating her curds and whey.
Along came a spider
And sat down beside her.
And then Miss Muffet went home.

When her students have gathered for the mini-lesson, Shirl says, "I've rewritten the nursery rhyme *Little Miss Muffet.* Listen to my boring ending." She reads the rhyme to the class, then continues, "Isn't that boring?! When we were writing leads, we said that writers sometimes experiment. Writers will also often try different ways to write an ending. Who can remember the three ways to make an appealing ending?" After students recall the three ways, the class chants the rhyming couplet. Shirl wants to help her students experiment with different ways to end her Miss Muffet rhyme. She's not concerned that they identify the type of ending; she just wants them to consider other options. She resumes her mini-lesson:

> I'm going to experiment and make up a different ending to replace my boring one. After the spider sat down beside her, maybe I could end with "Then that hungry spider gobbled up the curds and whey!" That's a new ending! Or I could write, "Miss Muffet jumped off her tuffet, grabbed a hammer, and squashed that nasty spider flat!" Put your thumbs up if you like my endings. Can anyone else experiment and try a new ending for Little Miss Muffet?

The students volunteer ideas for a new ending. The class concludes this lesson by chanting the rhyming couplet.

Other lessons on appealing endings will be spread throughout the school year. Primary students are unlikely to be developmentally ready to craft good endings on command; thus, no target practice accompanies this lesson sequence. As the year progresses, Shirl and her students will identify and chart the types of endings in books that they read. They will collect samples of appealing endings for the VOICES bulletin board. Often after a read-aloud book, Shirl will model experimenting with two or three other ending possibilities.

O = Onomatopoeia

When we introduce the VOICES category of onomatopoeia, we also include the skill of alliteration. We use "Splash! The duck dives deep into the pond" as a sample for both onomatopoeia and alliteration. We also use the picture of a duck in a pond as an accompanying illustration.

Shirl begins the lesson by holding up the O poster and saying, "Today we're going to learn another thing good writers use. It's called onomatopoeia. Isn't that a funny word? *Onomatopoeia* means using sound words to give the reader a better picture." She then holds up the other posters and continues:

> O stands for onomatopoeia. We'll also learn about alliteration in a few days. Here is a sentence that uses both onomatopoeia and alliteration: "Splash! The duck dives deep into the pond." What picture came into your brain when you heard those words?

As Shirl holds up the illustration, she says:

> Here is a picture to remind us to use sound words. It's just like the picture you saw in your brain. The word <u>splash</u> is onomatopoeia because it is the sound that the duck made when it went into the pond. When you listen to stories and poems, we're going to be searching for sound words. When you find one, you can hold up your fingers to make an O. Here's our rhyme for onomatopoeia. Hold up an O when you hear a sound word."

After saying the rhyming couplet (Figure 4-8), students return to their five-page books.

ONOMATOPOEIA

"Crash – bang – thump – screech – sizzle – tweet."
Onomatopoeia is a noisy treat.

Figure 4-8.   Rhyming Couplet for Onomatopoeia

The second mini-lesson begins with a review of the previous day's work. After chanting the rhyming couplet several times, Shirl says:

> Today we're going to make a chart on which we list all the onomatopoeia we hear. Let's sing the song "The Wheels on the Bus," and if you hear a sound word, make sure you hold up the O you make with your fingers. When we finish singing, we'll list the onomatopoeia that we hear.

After singing, students begin the chart with the object and the sound from the song (e.g., horn—beep; wipers—swish). Shirl's lesson continues; she has the students sing "Are You Sleeping?" and adds the onomatopoeia *ding dong* to the class chart.

The next day's lesson reviews the rhyming couplet and the onomatopoeia chart, and Shirl states,

> We're going to add onomatopoeia to a nursery rhyme. Let's use *Little Miss Muffet* to add some sound words. I'll do the first line. I think when <u>Little Miss Muffet</u> sat on her tuffet, it would make a squishing noise. So I'll write <u>squish</u> after the first line. What sound word could we use as Little Miss Muffet was eating her curds and whey?

The class brainstorms onomatopoeia for the rest of the nursery rhyme as follows:

> Little Miss Muffet sat on her tuffet (squish)
> Eating her curds and whey (slurp).
> Along came a spider who sat down beside her (plop),
> And frightened Miss Muffet away (screech).

Shirl continues, "Let's add some of these words to our onomatopoeia chart. Can you think of any other sound words that we could add to our chart?" When the students have suggested other words, Shirl introduces the target practice. Using the sample sentence "The doorbell went ding dong," Shirl directs the students to write their own sentence with the pattern "The ___ went ___." Students complete the target practice activity, then return to their five-page books. Shirl ends this writing workshop session by having several students share their target practice sentence; then she warns, "Onomatopoeia is lots of fun to use in our writing. It gets the readers' attention and makes our piece more interesting. But if you use too many sound words, your writing will be too noisy!"

After students have had these lessons on onomatopoeia, Shirl uses the skill to introduce another kind of lead. She begins:

> When we were first learning about VOICES, we learned that authors experiment with different leads to hook their reader into reading more. We've already learned that an author can

> use action as an interesting lead. Authors sometimes use ono-
> matopoeia as a lead, too. The onomatopoeia hooks readers so
> they keep on reading.

Shirl has the nursery rhyme *Five Little Monkeys Jumping on the Bed* on chart paper. She continues, "Let's use this nursery rhyme and change the lead by putting in a sound word. What might be the first word we could use as the little monkeys were jumping on the bed?" The class experiments with words such as *Boing!, Plop!,* and *Poof!* On subsequent days, Shirl revisits some of her writing to add onomatopoeia as a lead, and she supports students as they revisit their leads to add a sound word.

Alliteration

To begin the mini-lesson on alliteration, Shirl says:

> When we studied onomatopoeia, we learned that authors use
> sound words to help make their writing more interesting to
> their readers. Today we're going to learn about another way
> that authors use sounds to make their writing more interest-
> ing. It's called alliteration. Sometimes a writer will repeat a sound
> in two or three different words. Our rhyme for alliteration has
> a sound that repeats. Listen as I read our alliteration rhyme.

She reads the rhyming couplet (see Figure 4-9) and leads the class in a discussion of the alliteration within the rhyme. After chanting the rhyme several times, Shirl continues, "Today, we're going to write some alliteration using your names." Shirl asks a student to stand beside her. She guides students in thinking about action words and naming words that begin with the same sound as this student's name. With Shirl's help, the student then makes an alliterative sentence using his or her name (e.g., Sally slides in the sand; Bob bakes brownies; Jose honks the horn; Tom takes turns). Shirl guides the students in making several more alliterative sentences using their classmates' names. Finally, students get in knee-to-knee pairs and brainstorm other alliterative sentences using their partner's name. Students share some of their sentences with the class and then return to their five-page books.

ALLITERATION

Alliteration sounds so sweet.
It's a sound that does repeat.

Figure 4-9. Rhyming Couplet for Alliteration

The second lesson begins with a review of the rhyming couplet and the previous day's mini-lesson. Shirl says, "Today we're going to write some alliteration using animals. We'll write the alliteration on this chart so you can remember it and use it in your own writing." She guides the class in a discussion of alliteration using an animal and its movement (e.g., the cat crawls, the dog digs, the monkey marches). As Shirl writes the alliteration on the chart, students act out each sentence.

The next mini-lesson on alliteration follows the same pattern as the previous day. During this lesson, however, students expand their use of alliteration by brainstorming ordinary objects and describing their movements, number, and other qualities. Shirl gives several examples that she then writes on the alliteration chart (e.g., one windy winter, two tired turtles, a little lazy lizard). Students then make contributions to the chart. Shirl removes the chart from view and gives the target practice assignment. Students write and illustrate an alliterative phrase. For students who need additional help, Shirl confers with them in a small group, and they write an alliterative phrase together. Other students resume work on their five-page books.

After students have participated in several lessons related to alliteration, Shirl relates these lessons to good leads. Her lesson begins, "We've studied good leads before. Who can remember the two ways to make a good lead that we've already studied?" Once students recall using action and onomatopoeia to write a lead, she displays the nursery rhyme *Little Bo Peep* and continues:

> I'm going to experiment with a different lead for <u>Little Bo Peep</u>. I think I'll change Bo Peep's name to Little Lily Lou so her name makes an alliteration. So now my lead is "Little Lily Lou has lost her sheep." That's a pretty good alliteration. What if I changed the word <u>sheep</u> to <u>lambs</u>? That would be even better. How does this sound? *Little Lily Lou has lost her lambs and doesn'* I like that alliteration, and I think it makes the lead more interesting.

In subsequent days, Shirl revisits some of her writing to add an alliterative beginning, and she supports students as they revisit their leads to add alliteration.

I = Interesting Dialogue

When we introduce the VOICES category of interesting dialogue, we include the skills of dialogue and interjections. We use "'Wow! Look at that bug,' said Tom. Billy replied, 'It's a huge cricket'" as a sample for both dialogue and interjections. We also use the picture of two rabbits and a large cricket as an accompanying illustration.

The introductory lesson for dialogue begins with Shirl saying:

> Today we're going to be detectives. Detectives search for clues. As we read this big book, we're going to search for clues that people are talking. We call conversation in books <u>dialogue</u>. When we write, we want to use interesting dialogue to get the attention of our readers. The words that show talking are surrounded by quotation marks.

She introduces the sample sentence, icon, and rhyming couplet (Figure 4-10), and the class chants the rhyme several times. Using a big book, Shirl shows examples of dialogue and explains the necessary punctuation. (She uses *Mrs. Wishy Washy* by Joy Cowley [1980], but any big book with dialogue would be effective.) She continues, "As I read this big book to you, I want you to be a detective and let me know when you hear some dialogue. You'll hear the characters talking. When you hear it, make our dialogue sign with your hands." Shirl shows them how to make a V with two fingers on each hand and wiggle them up and down to show quotation marks. When students identify the dialogue, she uses highlighter tape to draw attention to the quotation marks.

INTERESTING DIALOGUE

You use dialogue to show conversation.
Then you add special punctuation.

Figure 4-10.   Rhyming Couplet for Interesting Dialogue

The second mini-lesson begins with a review of the rhyming couplet and the previous day's lesson. Shirl begins, "Today we're going to use the song 'Old MacDonald' to help us think about the special punctuation that we use when we write dialogue. Let's practice this chant to help us remember. 'Comma, quotation, capital, period, quotation.'" She writes the code for this chant (, " C . ") on a sentence strip as they chant together. Shirl explains that when we write dialogue, we first write who's talking, then put a comma, beginning quotation mark, capital letter, a period, and ending quotation mark. After reciting the chant several times, Shirl leads the class as they sing "Old MacDonald." Then Shirl continues:

> We're going to use this song to practice writing dialogue. We'll use this elbow macaroni and a frame sentence to practice the special punctuation used in dialogue. I'll show you what I mean. I think I'll write about the cow in "Old MacDonald." The cow says, "Moo." I'll draw a cow and use a speech bubble to show the cow saying, "Moo." Under my picture, I'll write my sentence and glue on this macaroni to show my quotation marks.

Shirl demonstrates (see Figure 4-11), and then passes out paper and macaroni for students to make their own picture and sentence based upon an animal from "Old MacDonald."

Prior to the third mini-lesson, Shirl prepares sentence strips with dialogue from familiar fairy tales. She leaves the speaker unidentified. Sentences include the following:

Figure 4-11. Practice with Dialogue

____ said, "I'll huff, and I'll puff, and I'll blow your house down."

____ said, "Someone's been sleeping in my bed."

____ said, "Grandma, what big eyes you have."

____ said, "You can't catch me!"

____ said, "Fee, fi, fo, fum. I smell the blood of an Englishman."

Shirl begins the lesson by reviewing the rhyming couplet and punctuation chant. She then says, "Today we're going to play a game called 'Who Said It?' I'm going to read some dialogue to you, and you have to think about who said it. Are you ready?" She reads each sentence strip, allows students to think about the speaker, and then writes the speaker's name to complete the sentence. After each sentence, she reviews the punctuation. Then Shirl assigns the target practice. She continues:

> For target practice today, I want you to write a sentence using this frame: ____ said, "____." You can use dialogue you might want to say to a friend, or dialogue you've heard from a favorite story. Remember to use the special punctuation. Comma, quotation, capital, period, quotation. You might want to try a strong verb in place of <u>said</u>. Here's my target practice: Mrs. Hawes said, "Do your best."

Shirl writes her sample sentence, highlights the punctuation, and then dismisses students to do their target practice and resume work in their five-page books.

After teaching several mini-lessons on dialogue, Shirl relates these lessons to good leads. Her lesson begins, "We've studied good leads before. We know that we can use action, onomatopoeia, or alliteration to hook our reader." She displays the nursery rhyme *Little Miss Muffet* and continues:

> I'm going to experiment with a different lead for <u>Little Miss Muffet</u>. I think I'll change the lead so that it uses dialogue. Dialogue is one kind of lead that writers use to hook their readers. Maybe the spider can be talking to Little Miss Muffet to begin the nursery rhyme. What would the spider say?

Students suggest phrases such as "Good morning," "Hello," and "I'm going to scare you." Then Shirl asks, "What would Miss Muffet say to the spider?" Students offer suggestions, and Shirl continues:

> We've made a new lead for <u>Little Miss Muffet</u> using dialogue. We might say, "Good morning," said the spider. "Get away from me!" said Little Miss Muffet as she sat on her tuffet eating her curds and whey. Now you know that when you begin a new piece, you can use action, onomatopoeia, alliteration, or dialogue to write an interesting lead to hook your readers.

In subsequent days, Shirl revisits some of her writing to experiment with leads using dialogue, and she supports students as they revisit their leads to add dialogue.

Interjections

Shirl's mini-lesson begins with an explanation of the meaning and function of interjections. She says:

> Today we're going to learn about interjections. I'll bet you use interjections all the time and never knew it. An interjection is something you say when you're surprised, happy, or mad. It shows your strong feelings. Interjections are words like "Oh, no!" or "Ouch!" or "Whee!" or "Ugh!" When you use an interjection, it makes your writing more exciting. To show our excitement, we usually put an exclamation mark after the interjection.

Shirl introduces the rhyming couplet (Figure 4-12), and the class chants it several times. Shirl continues:

> Over the next few lessons, we'll be working to understand interjections and use them in our writing. Today we'll start a list of any interjections that we already know. Let's see if we can find an interjection in the nursery rhyme <u>Three Little Kittens</u>.

Shirl presents the nursery rhyme on chart paper or a transparency, and she leads her class in identifying the word *oh* as an interjection. The class begins a list of interjections, adding *oh* to the list. The students are then dismissed to continue their five-page books.

INTERJECTIONS

"Wow!" cried the writer when he used an interjection.
"Making writing more exciting is a good suggestion."

Figure 4-12.   Rhyming Couplet for Interjections

Prior to the next day's mini-lesson, Shirl writes a poem containing several interjections onto a chart paper. (She uses "The Fourth" from Shel Silverstein's book *Where the Sidewalk Ends* [1974].) After reviewing the rhyming couplet, Shirl reads this poem and helps the students to identify and highlight the interjections. They add these words to the interjections list. Then she says:

> Now I'm going to give you a situation, and we'll all brainstorm the interjections we'd use. For example, if I dropped a glass, I might say, "Darn!" or "Oh, no!" or "Help!" I'll add those words to our chart. As I say the situation, raise your hand if you can think of an interjection you'd use. Then I'll add those words to our list.

Shirl gives situations such as the following:

- ✓ You skin your knee.
- ✓ You taste some food that's delicious.
- ✓ You taste some food that you don't like.
- ✓ You get a great present for your birthday.
- ✓ You see something amazing.
- ✓ You have a bad headache.
- ✓ You win a game.
- ✓ You go on a roller coaster.

As each interjection is offered, Shirl adds it to the chart, placing an exclamation mark after each one.

The third lesson on interjections uses the book by Ruth Heller entitled *Fantastic! Wow! and Unreal!: A Book About Interjections and Conjunctions* (1998). Shirl first reviews the rhyming couplet and interjections list, and then reads the first half of Heller's book. As she reads, she leads the class in a discussion of situations that might occur that would match some of the interjections in the book. Because the book tells that interjections change with the times, she shares some of the interjections that were popular when she was a child (like "groovy," "holy cow," and "outasight"). Shirl then explains the target practice assignment. She tells them to use an interjection from the chart to write and illustrate a sentence. Her sample sentences include "Oh no! I broke my mom's favorite vase" and "Whee! I love to ride on a roller coaster." Shirl releases the students to work on their target practice and their five-page books.

When the students have had several opportunities to learn about interjections, Shirl relates these mini-lessons to good leads. She begins, "We've studied good leads before. We know that we can use action, onomatopoeia, alliteration, or dialogue to hook our reader. Writers also can use an interjection as a lead to hook their readers." She displays the nursery rhyme *Wee Willie Winkie* on chart paper and reads it to the class. Shirl continues, "We know that Wee

Willie Winkie was running through town in his nightgown. What interjection could we use at the beginning?" Students offer suggestions such as "Wow!" and "Oh my!" and "Look!" Shirl writes their suggestions on stick-on notes and places them at the beginning of the nursery rhyme. In subsequent days, Shirl revisits some of her writing to experiment with leads using interjections, and she supports students as they revisit their leads to add an interjection.

C = Comparison

When we introduce the VOICES category of comparison, we include the skills of simile, metaphor, and personification. We use the sentences "The rain played a sad song on my head. My hair felt like a wet mop" as a sample for the three kinds of comparison, and we use an accompanying illustration.

Similes

To introduce comparisons, Shirl holds up the C poster and begins:

> This C stands for <u>comparison</u>. Good writers use comparison to show how two things are alike. They compare one thing to another thing. Here are the sentences that we will use to help us think about comparison. As I read our sentences, think about the picture you're getting in your brain. "The rain played a sad song on my head. My hair felt like a wet mop." What did you see in your brain?

The students talk about their mental images, and then Shirl hold up the accompanying illustration. She continues,

> In these sentences, I compare the rain to a musician who plays a sad song. I also compare hair to a wet mop because the rain makes me feel all wet and limp, just like a mop that's all wet. Today we'll study one kind of comparison called a <u>simile</u>. We are using a simile when we say that one thing is *like* another thing. Let's read our rhyming couplet and see what two things are being compared.

Shirl reads the simile rhyme (Figure 4-13), and the students chant it several times.

Shirl guides the class in understanding that the rhyme compares writing to a strong bear. She asks, "When we say, 'A simile makes writing as strong as a bear,' we are comparing our writing and a bear. How are these two things alike?" After a discussion, Shirl continues:

> That's right. Both our writing and a bear are strong. Our rhyming couplet uses a simile to help us compare strong writing to a strong bear. When we use a simile, we use either <u>like</u> or <u>as</u>. Now let's use the nursery rhyme <u>Twinkle, Twinkle, Little Star</u> to find another simile.

Shirl reads the nursery rhyme and helps the students to identify the two things that are compared (a star and a diamond) and how they are alike (they both twinkle or shine). To end this mini-lesson, Shirl reads several sentences that she's written on sentence strips. She guides the students as they identify the two things being compared and how they are alike. Her sentences include the following:

> The rabbit is as soft as a pillow.
>
> The giant was as tall as a mountain.
>
> My dad's face felt like sandpaper.

SIMILE

**When you use "like" or "as" to compare,
A simile makes writing as strong as a bear!**

Figure 4-13. Rhyming Couplet for Similes

To begin the second mini-lesson on similes, Shirl and her students read the rhyming couplet. They then recite the first verse of *Mary Had a Little Lamb* to identify the two things being compared (lamb's fur and snow) and how they are the same (they are both white). Shirl says:

> We are good at finding similes in other people's writing. Now we'll see if we can write some similes together. Today we'll use color words to compare two things. If I wanted to write about the red shirt I have on today, I could compare it to something else that's red. What are some things I could compare my shirt to?

The class brainstorms items that are red, and Shirl begins a simile chart by recording their ideas (e.g., as red as a sunburn, red like a tomato, as red as a Christmas ribbon). They then collaborate to create similes for color words to describe other items in the classroom, and Shirl records those on the chart, too. Examples include the following:

> The paper is as white as a marshmallow.
>
> His backpack is brown like chocolate.
>
> The door is as blue as the sky.
>
> The book is yellow like a lemon.

Students then return to their five-page books.

The next mini-lesson begins with a review of strong verbs. They chant the simile rhyming couplet, and then Shirl says:

> When we studied strong verbs, we named many words we could use to show how something moves. Today, we'll use those strong verbs to make similes. We'll name a way to move, and then compare the movement to something else. Here's one to start with: "I run like a ____." What could we compare the running to so that we finish the sentence?

The students brainstorm comparisons for Shirl's sentence and then create other similes with movements such as the following:

I wiggle like a _____.

I slither as fast as a _____.

I jump like a _____.

I spin like a _____.

As they chant each simile, the students act out the movement. Before sending the students to their seats, Shirl says:

> When you are writing, you don't want to use similes too often. Maybe you could use one or two similes in each book. If you use too many similes, your writing will be too busy! Now we'll try our target practice. I want each of us to write and illustrate a simile. I think I'll write about being cold. I'll say, "I am as cold as an ice cube." Then I'll draw myself shivering.

Shirl models the target practice with her simile and then has the students try the target practice assignment on their own.

Shirl and her students revisit the skill of simile at other times throughout the year. They make similes based on emotions, texture, size, taste, and temperature, and Shirl adds these comparisons to the class simile chart.

Metaphors

To begin the first mini-lesson on metaphor, Shirl introduces the rhyming couplet (Figure 4-14).

METAPHORS

A metaphor is a window into your book.
When you compare two things, you get a better look.

Figure 4-14. Rhyming Couplet for Metaphors

After the class chants it several times, Shirl continues:

> When we use a metaphor, we compare two things to see how they are alike, just as we did when we wrote similes. But metaphors are trickier because they don't use <u>like</u> or <u>as</u> to compare. In our rhyming couplet, we said that a metaphor is a window into a book. Of course, we know that a metaphor isn't really a window. We compare a metaphor to a window because they both give us a look. A window helps us to look into a building, and a metaphor helps us to look at a comparison. If I say, "My mom is a crab when she's mad," I don't mean that she's a real crab. I'm comparing my mom to a crab because they're both ferocious when they're mad! Now let's see if we can find a metaphor in a poem. Remember that a metaphor makes a comparison.

Any poem with an obvious metaphor is appropriate for use in this lesson. Shirl reads the poem "The Toaster" by William Jay Smith (Prelutsky, 1983). In this poem, Smith compares a toaster to "a silver-scaled dragon with jaws flaming red." Shirl and her students discuss what is being compared (a toaster and a dragon) and how they are alike (they both use fire). Next, Shirl holds up a stapler and continues:

> We've seen how William Jay Smith compares a toaster to a dragon. He used a metaphor to compare. Now let's try to use this stapler to write a metaphor. How is this stapler like an animal? What animal could we use to describe a stapler? What is the animal stapler doing to the paper?

As the students answer her questions, Shirl guides the students in brainstorming several examples of metaphor related to the stapler. Examples include the following:

A stapler is a greedy alligator snapping at a pile of papers.

A stapler is a tyrannosaurus chomping on two papers.

A stapler is a hungry wolf biting the paper's corner.

Shirl records the suggestions on chart paper, and then the students continue working on their five-page books.

The second mini-lesson begins with a review of the metaphor rhyming couplet. Shirl next asks the students to listen as she reads the nursery rhyme *Mary, Mary, Quite Contrary*. She says:

> This rhyme says that Mary's garden had silver bells and pretty maidens in it. Maidens are girls. Would bells and girls really be growing in a garden? No! What really grows in gardens? Yes, the rhyme is comparing the flowers in Mary's garden to bells and girls.

Shirl shows several pictures of flowers (from a seed catalog or downloaded from the Internet). The students discuss the similarities between flowers and silver bells, and between flowers and pretty girls all in a row. Shirl then holds up a pencil and asks:

> What do you think about when you see this pencil? Does it remind you of anything special? Think about the pencil's color, its shape, and how it moves. When we write a metaphor about this pencil, we want to relate this pencil to what it does—it writes words or draws pictures.

The students discuss possible comparisons, and Shirl helps them to hone their suggestions into metaphorical statements, which she adds to the chart paper from the previous day. Each example includes the pencil, the comparison, and a relationship to writing or drawing. Examples composed by her students include the following:

> A pencil is a yellow bus full of pictures.
>
> A pencil is a ballerina dancing across the paper.
>
> A pencil is a rocket shooting words into space.

The third mini-lesson on metaphor is an adaptation from the book *Teeth, Wiggly as Earthquakes* by Judith Tannenbaum (2000). After reviewing the rhyming couplet, Shirl begins by stating, "Today we'll write some metaphors by comparing ourselves to our favorite things. What are some things that you like a lot?" She writes these things on the board (e.g., animals, cartoon characters, toys, sports equipment, games, or places). She continues:

> To write a metaphor, I'm going to think about something that's a favorite of mine. I will compare myself to something I like. I really like to visit the ocean, so I could write, "I am a wild wave crashing against the shore." That sentence compares me to the ocean's wave. You know that I love hedgehogs, so I could write, "I am a prickly hedgehog curled up into a sleepy ball." What am I comparing in that sentence?

After discussion, Shirl says:

> I didn't just write, "I'm a hedgehog." I told *how* I was like a hedgehog. Now you're going to get knee to knee and try to make some metaphors with each other. You'll think about things you like, just as I did, and compare each other to those things. Remember to tell what you are doing in your metaphor!

Shirl moves from pair to pair, listening to their metaphors and supporting the partners who need help. After approximately 10 minutes have passed, students write and illustrate a metaphor for target practice and then return to their five-page books.

Personification

Shirl introduces the skill of personification by saying:

> Today we're going to learn one more way to write a compari-
> son. It's called <u>personification</u>. As I write the word on the board,
> you can see the word <u>person</u> hidden at the beginning. That
> will help you to remember what personification is. Personifica-
> tion allows a nonhuman character to act like a person. Let's
> learn our rhyme about personification.

Shirl reads the rhyming couplet (Figure 4-15), and the class chants it several times.

She continues:

> In this rhyme, the sun is acting like a human because it is smil-
> ing. In our comparison sentence "The rain played a sad song
> on my head," the rain is acting like a human because it is
> playing a sad song. Whenever a nonhuman character acts like
> a person, it's called <u>personification</u>. Now I'll read two nursery
> rhymes, and I want you to listen to see if you can identify the
> characters that act like humans.

She reads *Hey Diddle Diddle* and *The Three Little Kittens,* and the students discuss the personification within the two rhymes. They chant the rhyming couplet again and then return to their five-page books.

PERSONIFICATION

**"The sun smiles down on me" is personification.
To make animals and things act like people,
use your imagination.**

Figure 4-15. Rhyming Couplet for Personification

To prepare for the second lesson on personification, Shirl writes the poem "April Rain Song" by Langston Hughes on chart paper. (The poem can be found in many poetry anthologies.) After the class chants the rhyming couplet, Shirl asks the students to identify how the rain acts like a human (kissing and singing a lullaby). She then says, "Today we're going to write some sentences with personification. To write personification, we need to think about an object that will act like a human. Let's list some things that only people can do." The students brainstorm actions done by people, and Shirl writes their ideas on the board. Then she says:

> Now we're going to try to think about an object doing some-
> thing from this list. I'll try one. To write personification, I need
> to think about an object, an action word, and a human out-

> come—something only a human can do. We have the word
> <u>sings</u> on our list. I'll write about a caterpillar singing. "A cater-
> pillar sings a munching song as it crawls along the leaf." Can a
> caterpillar really sing a song? No! I've used personification to
> make my caterpillar do an action that only a human can really
> do. Let's try some together.

Shirl guides her students as they create expanded sentences with an object, an action word, and a human outcome. Examples include the following:

> This rock wonders how it got to be so small.
>
> A cloud paints castles in the sky.
>
> My pencil hopes that I will sharpen it soon.
>
> The book wants me to read it.

The next mini-lesson on personification begins with a review of the rhyming couplet. Shirl says to her students, "Now we'll sing *I'm a Little Teapot*. I want you to try to find the personification in this song. Raise your hand if you hear the teapot acting like a human." The students identify the personification (the teapot shouting, "Come tip me over and pour me out"). Shirl continues:

> Today we'll write some personification that uses dialogue. I'll
> write our dialogue on this chart. Remember that when we
> write dialogue, we show that our character says something. It
> has special punctuation: comma, quotation, capital, period,
> quotation. To do this activity, we'll think of what an object
> might say if it were human. What would a spoon say?

Students offer suggestions, and Shirl writes them on the chart. Examples include the following:

> The spoon screamed, "Your ice cream is melting all over me!"
>
> The spoon sighed, "I can't wait to dive into the bowl of ice cream."
>
> The spoon screeched, "This soup is too hot!"

Shirl and her students consider other dialogue for inanimate objects (What would a pencil say? A vacuum cleaner? A mirror? A car? A flower?) After brainstorming several ideas for each object, Shirl assigns the target practice. Students write and illustrate a sentence with dialogue in which an object talks like a human.

After Shirl has introduced simile, metaphor, and personification, she relates these three forms of comparison to good leads. She begins:

> We've talked a lot about good leads before. We know that we
> can use action, onomatopoeia, alliteration, dialogue, or inter-
> jection to hook our reader. Writers also use comparison to hook
> their readers. They might use a simile, metaphor, or personifi-
> cation as a lead.

She displays the nursery rhyme *There Was an Old Woman Who Lived in a Shoe* on chart paper and reads it to the class. Shirl continues:

> Let's see if we can experiment with the beginning of this nursery rhyme by using a comparison to tell how old the lady was. Maybe we could say, "There was a woman as old as a dinosaur." What else can you think of that's really old that we could compare the old woman to?

The students offer suggestions, such as "old as the earth" or "old as a mummy." In subsequent days, Shirl revisits some of her writing to experiment with leads using a comparison, and she supports students as they revisit their leads to add a simile, metaphor, or personification.

E = Expand One Idea

When we introduce the VOICES category of expanding one idea, we also include the skills of narrowing the topic, using transition words, and writing with emotion. We use the sentences "Suddenly, a door creaked open. Out slithered an enormous dragon" as a sample for this category. We also use an accompanying illustration. In addition, we use a balloon throughout these lessons as a metaphor for expansion. We tell the students that boring writing is like a balloon that hasn't been blown up. Just like a balloon, writing is better when it's expanded.

Narrow the Topic

Shirl begins this mini-lesson near the overhead projector as she first introduces the E and the skills posters, sample sentence, and icon. She then tells her students, "I'm going to write about my weekend." She begins to write on a transparency:

> I went to Dallas this weekend. I went to a teachers' meeting. I went with my friend Debbie. We got lost on our way there. Debbie's mother made cookies for us to take with us. I learned a lot at the meeting. Then we drove back to Houston.

Shirl stops and rereads, then says:

> You know, that sounds kind of boring. It seems more like a list, and it doesn't have many details. I have a lot of little stories that I could write that tell about my trip to Dallas. I think I'll try to narrow my topic. When we narrow a topic, we pick one small piece of a big idea. I could write about staying with Debbie's mom on our trip, or I could write about talking with Debbie on our drive to Dallas. I could write about what I learned at the teachers' meeting. I think I've decided to narrow my topic and write about one part of my trip—getting lost on the way to the meeting.

Shirl introduces the rhyming couplet (Figure 4-16) by acting it out. She begins by spreading her arms apart and bringing them close together as she says, "Narrow your topic." When she says, "Write about one thing," she holds up one finger. Shirl wags her finger back and forth as she continues, "You don't have to write about everything." As she says the final word, Shirl again spreads her arms apart. Her students act out the rhyming couplet each time they chant it.

NARROW THE TOPIC

Narrow your topic. Write about one thing.
You don't have to tell about everything.

Figure 4-16.   Rhyming Couplet for Narrowing the Topic

Shirl then displays the nursery rhyme *Jack and Jill*. She reads it and then says:

> This nursery rhyme doesn't tell all about Jack and Jill's day. It doesn't say what they had for breakfast, or what they did at school, or what chores they did at home. The writer of this nursery rhyme narrowed the topic and wrote about only one thing that Jack and Jill did. As we write, we want to think about narrowing our topics, too.

They review the rhyming couplet, and then the students continue on their five-page books.

Expanding One Idea

This mini-lesson immediately follows the one on narrowing the topic. Shirl wants to help her students understand that once a writer has narrowed the topic, one idea needs to be expanded to help readers understand the topic better. Shirl begins by reviewing the previous day's lesson.

> We've learned that writers often narrow their topic instead of writing about everything that happened. I decided to write about my trip to Dallas, but I decided that it would be more interesting if I just wrote about a small moment instead of the whole trip. I'm going to begin my five-page book now about how Debbie and I got lost on our way to the teachers' meeting. Before I write, though, I want to think about my ideas. I can't just say, "Debbie and I got lost on our way to a meeting." That's not enough information for my readers! I want to give enough useful information so the reader will have a clear idea of what's happening in my piece. I have a rhyme that will help us to know how to give useful information. The rhyme is called "Expand One Idea." <u>Expand</u> means to make bigger. When I

> blow up a balloon, I expand it. When I write, I want to take a small idea and make it bigger.

Shirl introduces the rhyming couplet (see Figure 4-17), and the class chants it several times.

EXPAND ONE IDEA

When you expand one idea with useful information—like "who, what, where, when, how, and why"—you'll improve communication.

Figure 4-17. Rhyming Couplet for Expanding One Idea

On chart paper, Shirl lists "who, what, where, when, how, why." She says, "These words from our rhyme will help me to think about expanding my idea. I'll fill in the chart with useful information that will help me write my piece." (Shirl's chart is shown in Table 4-3.) After she completes the chart, she continues, "Now I've got some useful information that will help me to expand one idea." As usual, the students return to their five-page books once this lesson is completed.

The next day's mini-lesson begins with Shirl displaying the children's book *The Paperboy* (Pilkey, 1996). (Any book about a small moment would be appropriate.) She says:

> Let's look at how a published author has narrowed his topic and expanded on one idea. This book is about a boy who delivers papers. The author could have written about the boy's whole day. Instead, the author has narrowed the topic. The book is about only one small moment of the boy's day. The idea is expanded so that the reader learns useful information about the boy's morning paper deliveries.

Table 4-3. Expanding One Idea

Who	Debbie and I
What	got lost on our way to a teachers' meeting
Where	on the freeway in downtown Dallas
When	early one morning when traffic was very heavy
How	We thought we knew where we were going.
Why	We didn't look at a map or read the signs carefully.

After Shirl reads the book, they discuss the author's craft and read the rhyming couplets related to narrowing the topic and expanding one idea. The students continue working on their five-page books.

Target practice is done after the class has taken a field trip to the zoo. (Any interesting shared experience is appropriate for this lesson.) Shirl models how to make a time line of the events that she remembers from their field trip. Students then make their own time lines based on their personal memories of the trip. Shirl encourages students to select the most memorable event from their time lines so that they can expand this idea orally. She pairs students together for knee-to-knee discussions to recall details of who, what, where, when, how, and why in order to expand their idea. Shirl suggests that students pretend to be watching a video of that moment in their head, and they should tell their partner everything that is happening. To monitor the oral target practice, Shirl moves from group to group, assessing and guiding their discussions. Once students have rehearsed their expanded ideas, Shirl passes out paper, and students compose short pieces about their memorable event.

Using Transition Words

Shirl's next mini-lesson involves writing a draft of her "Losing the Way" piece that she's discussed before. She begins:

> I know that I want to write about my trip to Dallas when Debbie and I lost our way, and I've expanded my idea to give useful information to my readers. Now I'm going to start my piece on this transparency before I begin my five-page book. As I write, listen to see if you can give me some advice for making my piece better.

Shirl writes:

> Debbie and I were driving to the meeting in Dallas. And then we noticed that we were lost. And then we said, 'Oh, no! Where are we?' And then we looked around and noticed that we were driving away from our meeting place. And then we had to turn around. And then we drove through the busy streets. And then we were still lost. And then we got out a map and found our way to our meeting.

Shirl asks her students, "Do you have any advice for making my piece better?" Shirl accepts ideas until someone says that *and then* has been used too often. She continues:

> That's right. I keep writing, "and then . . . and then . . . and then." How boring! My reader would probably fall asleep! I need to use other transition words. Transition words are words we can use in place of <u>and then</u>, like <u>next</u>, <u>first</u>, or <u>suddenly</u>. Transition words help a reader to move smoothly from one idea to another. They tell when or where something happened. I have a rhyme that will help us to learn about transition words.

Shirl introduces the rhyming couplet (Figure 4-18), and the class chants it several times. She then says, "Tomorrow we'll begin a list of words we can use in place of *and then* so our readers won't be snoring!"

TRANSITION WORDS

"And then," "and then," "and then," "and then" gets a
little boring. Use other transition words so your
readers won't be snoring!

Figure 4-18. Rhyming Couplet for Transition Words

The next day, the class reviews the rhyming couplet for transition words. Then Shirl says:

> When we use transition words, we tell either when something happened or where something happened. Today we're going to learn about transition words that tell us about time. These words tell us when something happened. I've started a chart with some time words that we can use as we write. We might use words like today, yesterday, on Saturday, or first. Usually the time transition words are found at the beginning of a sentence. Listen as I read a couple of nursery rhymes, and give me a thumbs up when you hear words that tell when something happened.

Shirl reads several nursery rhymes with transition words related to time (e.g., *Hickory Dickory Dock, Old Mother Hubbard, Wee Willie Winkie*), and then the class brainstorms other time transitions to add to the chart (Table 4-4). For target practice, Shirl has her students write and illustrate a sentence that uses a time transition word. Her example is "Yesterday we went to the beach."

Table 4-4. Transition Words Chart

Time Words	Location Words
On Saturday	Above
Today	Across
Yesterday	Behind
Tomorrow	Up
One day	Under
Suddenly	Below
First	Beside
Next	Between
Last	Inside
Last Thursday	On top of

Shirl begins the next mini-lesson reviewing the rhyming couplet and the chart with time transition words. She continues:

> We know some transition words that tell us when something happened, and today we're going to learn about transition words that tell us where something happened. These are called location words because they tell us where something is located. Location transition words are usually found at the end of a sentence.

As in the lesson on time transition words, Shirl introduces several location words on a chart, reads some nursery rhymes with location words (e.g., *Jack and Jill, Little Miss Muffet, Humpty Dumpty*), and then guides the class as they create a chart with location transition words (see Table 4-4). She uses a puppet to act out some of the words to help students visualize the various locations. Before returning to their five-page books, the class completes a target practice by writing and illustrating a sentence that uses a location transition word. Shirl's example is "I saw a little mouse under the table."

Writing With Emotions

To help students use emotion in their writing, Shirl begins, "Writers often try to make their readers have emotion when they read. *Emotion* means feelings. Writers want their readers to feel happy, sad, scared, or mad." She reads the emotions rhyming couplet (see Figure 4-19), and the class chants it several times. She continues, "Today we're going to talk about things that make us happy. When we're happy, we feel good and we often laugh. Let's think about things that make us laugh or smile." Shirl reads several humorous poems (Shel Silverstein's or Jack Prelutsky's are class favorites) or revisits favorite stories to discuss the happy emotions that they evoke. She then pairs students for knee-to-knee discussions to brainstorm things that have made each student happy.

EMOTIONS

Happy, sad, scared, mad—how will your readers feel? When you write with emotions, your writing will seem real.

Figure 4-19. Rhyming Couplet for Emotions

The next three days of the emotions mini-lessons follow the same sequence as the lesson on happy emotions. Shirl first teaches about sad emotions, then scary emotions, and finally emotions of anger. For each mini-lesson, the class first reviews the emotions rhyming couplet, reads or reviews stories and poems with emotions, and then gets knee to knee to discuss emotional moments.

For the last day's lesson on emotions, Shirl gives a target-practice assignment. She gives each student a half-sheet of writing paper and tells them to write a short story that makes the reader feel an emotion. She sets a timer for 10 minutes and then collects the papers. After calling the class to the large-group area, she reads several of their pieces aloud. As each piece is read, she asks the students to determine which emotion they felt. The class discusses whether each piece evoked a happy, sad, scary, or angry emotion. The lesson ends as the class chants the emotions rhyming couplet.

During the week(s) that these lessons are taught, Shirl connects these writing workshop skills to books read aloud. After each read-aloud opportunity, the students discuss how the story made them feel. To increase their awareness of each writer's craft, Shirl helps the students to identify the words and techniques that each writer uses to bring forth a particular emotion in their readers.

S = Specificity

When we introduce the VOICES category of specificity, we include the skills of using descriptive words (number, color, size, and material words) and proper nouns. We use the sentence "Rover found two big bones under the wooden table" as a sample for all the skills within this category. We also, as always, use an accompanying illustration.

Descriptive Words

To begin instruction in this category, Shirl first introduces the visual aids that accompany this VOICES category. She then says:

> When you write a piece, you need to give specific information so that the readers get a crystal-clear picture in their brains. When you're specific, you give exact details. Let's try a little game so you can see what I mean. In your brain, picture a dog. What did you see?

The students discuss the many types of dogs they visualized. Shirl continues:

> We all saw different kinds of dogs because just saying "a dog" isn't very specific. Now picture in your mind a black-and-white dog. That's a little more specific. We know the dog is black and white, but we still don't know specifically what kind of dog it is. Is it little? Is it big? Does it have a black body and a white face, a white body with black spots, or black-and-white stripes? How long is its tail? We just don't know. Now I will be more specific. Picture in your mind an enormous Dalmatian. Now we know that the dog is black and white. We know that it's big, and because it's a Dalmatian we know that it is white with small black spots. When we just pictured a dog in our minds, we didn't have enough details to get an exact picture, but

> when we pictured Dalmatian, our minds knew exactly what
> was described. That's what it means to be specific. We give
> exact details so our readers can know exactly what our writing
> is describing. Tomorrow we'll start talking about ways to be
> more specific in our writing.

Shirl tells her students to return to their five-page books.

The second mini-lesson begins as Shirl introduces the rhyming couplet for descriptive words, and she has the students chant it (Figure 4-20).

She then reads the Mother Goose rhyme *Baa, Baa, Black Sheep,* written on chart paper. She says, "This nursery rhyme will help us to think about being specific. It has some number, size, color, and materials words in it. Let's see if we can find a number word, and we'll use this tape to highlight it." They then use highlighter tape (you could also use a highlighter marker) to highlight first the number words within the rhyme (*three* bags full) and then the color word (*black* sheep). Shirl reminds her students that they have number and color charts already displayed in their classroom. The students complete the target practice by writing and illustrating a sentence that uses both a number and a color word.

DESCRIPTIVE WORDS

Add number, size, and color words to be more specific. Also add material words. Your writing will be terrific.

Figure 4-20.   Rhyming Couplet for Descriptive Words

The next lesson begins with a review of the rhyming couplet, and then Shirl helps the students to focus on size words. They highlight the size word in *Baa, Baa, Black Sheep* (*little* boy who lives down the lane). The class brainstorms words related to size, and Shirl records these words on a chart. Finally, students write and illustrate a sentence that uses a size word for target practice.

For the final mini-lesson, the students revisit the rhyming couplet and highlight the material word (*wool*) in *Baa, Baa, Black Sheep.* Shirl shares swatches of different fabrics because most of her students haven't been exposed to the terms used to describe these materials. Then students take turns walking around the room and touching items made of different materials. Each student orally creates a sentence related to the material that he or she has touched (e.g., a *wooden* table). Finally, the class begins a chart to list different material words to describe houses (wooden, brick, steel), clothing (silk, denim, cotton), and jewelry (ruby, gold, diamond). As target practice, Shirl asks the students to write and illustrate a sentence that uses a material word. After students have completed their target practice, they return to their five-page books.

Proper Nouns

Shirl introduces this writing skill by beginning with the rhyming couplet (Figure 4-21). She says, "Today's rhyme is about using proper nouns to be more specific. A proper noun is the name of a person or a place. Let's say our rhyme together."

PROPER NOUNS

Be a name dropper.
Use a noun that is proper.

Figure 4-21. Rhyming Couplet for Proper Nouns

After the class reads the rhyme several times, Shirl continues:

> I could write about my friend, but I'm more specific if I give my friend's name—Dawn. I could write about my visit to the doctor, but I'm more specific when I use a proper noun—Dr. Wolf. I could write about the city I live in, but instead of saying <u>city</u>, I could say <u>Houston</u>. Using a proper noun makes my writing more specific.

Just as she did during her initial lessons on number, color, size, and material words, Shirl helps her students to show that using a proper noun enables the brain to get a more exact picture. She uses the following sentence sequence:

Mom went to the store.

Mom went to the grocery store.

Mom went to Wal-Mart Supercenter.

The class uses these sentences to discuss how the proper noun gives the reader a better picture of where Mom went shopping. After they chant the rhyming couplet again, Shirl reminds her students to look for proper nouns in their reading and writing. Students then continue working on their five-page books.

The second mini-lesson on proper nouns begins with a review of the previous day's lesson and a recitation of the rhyming couplet. Shirl then uses a familiar nursery rhyme to show the difference that a proper noun makes. She says, "I know you like the nursery rhyme *Humpty Dumpty*." The class says the nursery rhyme together. Shirl continues, "Let's see how it would sound without a proper noun. 'The egg sat on the wall. The egg had a great fall. All the king's horses and all the king's men couldn't put the egg together again.'" She leads the class in a discussion about how the rhyme is more interesting and specific with the proper noun added. Next, Shirl places an unlit candle in a candlestick on the floor and recites the nursery rhyme *Jack Be Nimble.* She says, "We can use this nursery rhyme to have some fun with proper nouns. When we say the rhyme with your proper name instead of Jack's, you can stand up and move around the candlestick." Shirl takes this opportunity to review strong verbs by discussing alternatives for the word *jump.* Each child chooses a strong verb and the class chants the nursery rhyme with the strong verb (e.g., "Mary be nimble, Mary be quick, Mary slithered around the candlestick"). As their rhyme is chanted, each child acts it out.

After reciting the rhyming couplet, Shirl begins the third mini-lesson by beginning a proper-noun chart and brainstorming specific names for each category (Table 4-5). (The category options are numerous; choose the ones that will interest your students.) Shirl uses this occasion to reinforce students' use of capital letters for proper nouns. The class will continue to add to the chart throughout the year. The lesson ends with target practice. Shirl directs the students to write a sentence that uses proper nouns. Her sample sentence is "On Sunday, Mary drove to Wal-Mart." She tells her students they can use the frame sentence "On ____, ____ drove to ____" if they choose. When students are finished with target practice, they continue working on their five-page books.

Table 4-5.   Categories of Proper Nouns

Stores	Restaurants	Cities	Countries	Book Characters	Friends

Sustaining VOICES

The lessons we've described in this chapter will require many opportunities for reinforcement and encouragement so that students begin to use the skills in their own writing. During any of the VOICES lessons, a few students will only be at the recognition stage of development; that is, they can recognize the skill in the books they read but they aren't yet ready to use them routinely in their writing. Most students will recognize the VOICES skills and use them often, sometimes with reminders from you. You'll even have a few students who gobble up the ideas presented in this chapter and overuse them. That's okay—as they grow as writers, they'll develop more maturity in their writing and use the skills more judiciously.

Our VOICES structure provides a framework in which to introduce and discuss concepts related to the author's craft, and it helps teachers to guide their young writers as the students develop their writing skills. However, the lessons alone will not be enough to keep the ideas foremost in students' minds as they write. Instead, to sustain the VOICES skills, teachers must keep them alive. We can do this by locating them in familiar books, modeling their use through our own writing, revisiting them in mini-lessons, and using did-it dots. We can celebrate with our students when we see the VOICES skills used in their writing. As primary teachers, we won't see our students become sophisticated authors who write with complex plots. However, we will hear their own voices shine through in their writings as we work to maintain their understanding of VOICES.

Chapter

5

Adaptations
and Support Structures

Effective teaching is based on continuous decision-making by a
professional in response to the current context of the classroom.
Thoughtful decisions are well informed through experience and
knowledge, but they are made in response to individual children
in particular settings at given moments in time.

—Carol Avery, *And With a Light Touch*

Debbie works in an at-risk school. The students she works with come from homes with limited financial resources, few books, and, often, limited time to support the school's efforts. Many of the students do not speak English at home. Sometimes these students arrive in the United States with no schooling at all. They initially struggle with some of the writing tasks Debbie assigns. However, because of the adaptations and support structures available during writing workshop, Debbie is able to meet the individual needs of all learners.

Both of us make concerted efforts throughout the year to produce fluent and capable writers. These efforts include helping writers to identify signals to the reader, making meaningful connections to literature, and listening to poetry to show how writers write about ordinary things. In addition, students participate in interactive writing lessons, phonics lessons, and word wall activities. Finally, for struggling students, we provide instructional modifications to ensure each student's success.

In this chapter, we will share adaptations and support structures that we have found helpful as we've worked to raise young writers. We will identify activities for beginning the year with novice writers, discuss adaptations to our five-page book format for kindergarten writers, suggest modifications for struggling writers, and share an instructional format for spelling and word study.

Beginning the Year With Beginners

Rationale

As a first-grade teacher, Shirl realized that although most of her students were exposed to writing in kindergarten, they needed explicit instruction in some of the fundamental concepts that serve as prerequisites to a successful writing workshop. So instead of launching directly into the writing workshop format described in chapter 2, Shirl begins her year with approximately 6 weeks of lessons that will serve as a foundation for future work during writing workshop. These lessons are also appropriate for kindergartners as they begin writing workshop.

First Mini-Lessons

On the first two days of school, Shirl conducts several basic lessons. She gathers a writing sample for each student and models how to write her name and the date on paper. For each child, she prepares a "journal," a booklet made from about 20 sheets of unlined paper inside a construction-paper cover. The journal will be used for most of the activities she conducts during her beginning-of-the-year writing lessons.

On the first day of school, prior to any writing lessons, Shirl asks her students to write on a topic of their choice. She passes out unlined paper for students to use as they complete this task. Some students will resist the task because they are inexperienced writers or lack confidence in their writing skills. Shirl simply tells them that whatever they do is okay; she just wants to see what they can do so she knows what they need to learn. This writing sample then serves two purposes. It helps Shirl to identify the writing strengths and needs of each student. It also serves as a benchmark so that Shirl can ascertain the writing progress of each child as she compares future writing to the benchmark paper.

Target skill: Name on paper. Also on the first day of school, Shirl models how she expects students to write their names on their papers. For every assignment she gives them, Shirl first demonstrates how to write her name on her paper. She assists students as they then write their own names.

Target skill: Name and date. On the second day of school, Shirl passes out the "journals" she has constructed. Using her own journal as a model, Shirl shows the students how to put their name and the day's date at the top of the first sheet. She then writes the date on the board, using a consistent location throughout the school year. As students write their name and the date on the first page of their journal, Shirl monitors, assists, and rewards with did-it dots. It now becomes expected that students will use this target skill for all papers during the year.

Signals to the Reader

To help students identify concepts related to written language, Shirl utilizes a big book and the 20-page journal to introduce "signals to the reader." These signals, such as left-to-right progression and spaces between words, are used by writers to help their readers make meaning. Shirl reviews the signals daily, but she doesn't expect all the students to use them routinely at first. After daily modeling and repetition of the signal language, her students start to include each signal when they are developmentally ready. Shirl teaches one target skill per day, beginning on the third day of school.

Target skill: Letters and words. To introduce signals to the reader, Shirl begins:

> Everything we do when we write is a signal to the reader. We tell the reader what to do. We tell the reader when a new sentence is starting. We tell the reader when the sentence is over. Readers expect all writers to do certain things to help them read books. Today in writing workshop, we are going to start learning these signals so we can help our readers. We'll call these "signals to the reader."

Shirl displays an easy big book and asks, "When you're reading a book, how do you know what to read?" She leads the students in determining that the book contains words and letters that tell the reader the message. Shirl then turns to her journal, verbalizes the sentence she wants to write, and says, "As I write, I want to use letters and words." She writes her sentence in her journal and illustrates it. For this lesson, she uses conventional spelling because she's not yet ready to model spelling strategies. After passing out the journals and reminding students to first write their names and the date, she monitors as they are writing to ensure that they are using letters and words.

Target skill: Strategies to spell. Shirl begins this lesson by saying, "When writers write, they have to spell words. No one knows how to spell every word there is, so we have to use strategies to spell words we don't know. A strategy is a plan." Shirl continues by verbalizing the sentence she wants to write, and she turns to her journal. She illustrates her sentence first and then writes several of the words. She looks puzzled as she comes to a word she wants to spell using a spelling strategy. "When I don't know how to spell a word, there are a couple things I can try. I can look around the room and at the word wall to see if I can find the word I need." She looks at the word wall (which has only a few words introduced in kindergarten and the first day of school) and copies the word she needs. Shirl continues writing her sentence and again looks puzzled as she comes to another word that she wants to spell using sound-spelling. "I can't find the word I need on the word wall or anywhere around the room, so I'm going to use "turtle talk." She explains that turtles do things very slowly, so *turtle talk* means to talk as a turtle would. She models by saying a sentence slowly. "I a-m y-ou-r f-ir-s-t g-r-a-de t-ea-ch-er. I've just turtle-talked!" Shirl and her students practice turtle talk with several more sentences, then she turns back to her journal. She finishes her sentence by spelling with turtle talk and then instructs the students to use spelling strategies when they don't know how to spell a word.

Target skill: Left to right. Using the big book, Shirl asks, "When you are reading a book, where do you expect the author to write the first word? Then where does the next word go?" Shirl shows that the author of the big book started on the left and moved to the right. The class confirms this pattern by checking one or two more pages. Then Shirl turns to her journal. She writes a simple sentence, showing that her text begins on the left and moves to the right.

Target skill: Spaces between words. To model spacing between words, Shirl begins, "When a writer is finished with one word and needs to write the next word, what do we expect him or her to do between each word?" Using the big book, Shirl shows the students that there are spaces between each word. The students confirm this practice by checking other pages. As she does with many lessons, Shirl has a kinesthetic component to this target skill. She holds up one hand with her fingers spread widely. She uses her fingers to correspond to words and the spaces between her fingers to represent the spaces between words (Figure 5-1).

Next, Shirl uses her journal to write her name and the date and to review beginning on the left and moving to the right. She then writes a simple sentence and stresses leaving a space between words. She uses a finger or a Popsicle stick to highlight the space. When students receive their journals, Shirl reminds them to start on the left ("Where should you start your first word?") and to put a space between each word. As she monitors, she passes out Popsicle sticks so that students have a tool to help them leave spaces.

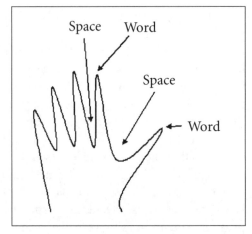

Figure 5-1. Representation for Spacing Between Words

Target skill: Return sweep. The lesson format continues for the remaining four lessons: an introduction to the skill, locating its use in a big book, teacher modeling, and student practice. Shirl begins, "When an author has filled up the first line of the paper but needs to write more words, where do we expect the words to go now?" She uses the big book to show return sweep ("go under and over to the left") and then confirms it on other pages. In her journal, Shirl models by writing a sentence that requires a return sweep. She reviews prior target skills and monitors as students write.

Target skill: Periods. To begin this lesson, Shirl states, "What do we expect the author to put at the end of a sentence to show us that the sentence is finished?" As usual, she uses a big book to show periods at the end of each sentence. Turning to her journal, she writes a short sentence, including left-to-right progression, spaces, and a period at the end. Next, she writes a second, related sentence that requires a return sweep. She asks her students, "Since I'm out of room, what do I do now?" She demonstrates putting a period at the end of the sentence rather than at the end of the line. Finally, Shirl monitors students as they write, reminding them to put a period at the end of the sentence. (This is the first of many lessons on punctuation. Students will need a great deal of modeling and support before they accurately use periods. Later lessons will also include other types of punctuation.)

Target skill: Lowercase letters. Shirl asks, "When an author writes a sentence, do we expect to see mostly capital letters or mostly lowercase letters?" She uses a big book to show that most of the letters are lowercase. She then writes a sentence in her journal that includes a mixture of a few capital letters and mostly lowercase letters. She also reviews previously addressed target skills. When her sentence is complete, she rereads it and says, "Oops! I have some mixed-up capital and lowercase letters. I need to fix my writing so I don't confuse my reader. I need to take out some of those capital letters and replace them with lowercase letters." Shirl then scans for any capital letters, crosses them out, and writes lowercase letters above them. As students work on their own journal entries, Shirl monitors and supports. (Future lessons will demonstrate that an author sometimes capitalizes all the letters in a word for emphasis or if it should be read in a loud voice.)

Target skill: Capital letter at the beginning. To begin this lesson, Shirl reminds the students of the target skill from the day before. "Yesterday we noticed that writers use mostly lowercase letters. Where do we expect to always see a capital letter?" She uses the big book to show that each sentence begins with a capital letter. She then models in her journal, writing a sentence that starts with a capital letter, progresses left to right, has a space between words, and ends with a period. As students write, Shirl checks their work and helps as needed. (Later in the year, mini-lessons will focus on the use of capital letters for the word "I" and for proper nouns.)

Treasure Books

When Shirl completes her "signals to the reader" lessons, she and her students move on to treasure books. In chapter 1, we gave you a brief introduction to treasure books—an alternative form of a journal. Shirl expects each of her students to bring a black-and-white composition book, which is sturdy enough to last the entire year and chronicle each child's growth as a writer. (If these composition books aren't available, you can continue making journals out of either unlined or lined paper and construction-paper covers.)

Prior to the first treasure-book lesson, Shirl prepares a writing folder for each student. These are similar to the folders that Debbie uses with her second graders, described in chapter 2. Shirl also prepares four separate charts, each with one of the following headings: People Writers Know, Things Writers Have, Places Writers Go, and Things Writers Do. As a special bonus (you might not have this option), Shirl gathers her old journals and her daughter's journal from kindergarten.

Introducing treasure books. Shirl introduces treasure books by stating, "Every moment in our lives is a treasure worthy of being written down." She shares her old journals—especially the empty pages, where she didn't write. She continues, "Because I didn't write every day in my treasure book, I have so many memories that are lost forever." She shares her daughter's journal from kindergarten and reads several entries. Shirl then says, "My treasure book is a place where I can write my memories. I will do my best, and I will keep it forever so I'll always have those memories to treasure." During this lesson, Shirl doesn't model. She directs the students to retrieve their own treasure books and write their name, the date, and a sentence (or sentences), and then illustrate it.

Thinking about authors' work. After the introductory treasure-book lesson, Shirl begins focusing on the work of writers. Her objective is to help her students understand that authors generally write about ordinary things, and they get inspiration from things in their own lives. Shirl will spend approximately 1 week for each of these topics: people writers know, things writers have, places writers go, and things writers do. We'll share the lesson sequence for the first topic. The lessons follow a similar sequence for each of the four topics.

Shirl begins, "Authors write about ordinary things. They often will write about people they know. Let's think about whom we know, and we can add those people to this chart." Shirl displays the People Writers Know chart and asks her students to brainstorm all the many people they know. As she writes on the chart, Shirl prompts as needed to expand the list. She continues:

> I have a new folder for each of you that we'll call our <u>writing folder</u>. The folder has pages that we'll use during writing workshop. The first page says, "Topics I Can Write About." I want all of you to take your new folder and open to the first page. Then I want you to write the names of people who make good memories for you.

Shirl first models in her own writing folder, and then students record the names of people of whom they have good memories.

On the second day of this lesson sequence, Shirl gathers some children's books or poems in which the authors have written about someone they know. (Table 2-2 lists some possible titles. You may want to consult with your school librarian as you gather these books.) Each day, she tries to find books or poems for one of the topics that correspond with ideas from the People Writers Know chart. For example, if one of the ideas on the chart is "sister," Shirl finds one or two books or poems featuring sisters. Before the second day's lesson begins, she also thinks of two or three stories about her own sister that she can share with the students.

She begins the lesson on the second day by stating, "Yesterday we made a list of many of the people we know. We learned that authors write about people they know. One of our ideas was 'sisters.' Here are two books that are written about sisters." Shirl shows the covers of the books, shares a brief synopsis of each, and then begins to tell her personal stories of her own sister:

> I have a sister I might write about. I could write about how my sister and I went shopping in the rain, or when she baked beautiful cakes for my children's birthdays, or about the time she had appendicitis and was in the hospital and I was so jealous because she got presents.

Shirl selects one of the ideas about her sister and writes several sentences in her treasure book. While modeling, she talks aloud as she writes, making sure that she mentions all the signals to the reader so that students are reminded daily. She also models the spelling strategies of sound-spelling and using the word wall. (Many times, Shirl begins her treasure-book entry and then sends the students off to write on their own. She sits with the students and quickly finishes her piece so they see her writing while they are working.) After modeling, Shirl reminds the students that they can choose their own topic or write about someone they know in their treasure book, and she sends them back to their seats to begin.

On each of the subsequent three days, Shirl selects another topic from the People Writers Know list. She shares literature samples, models a treasure-book entry on the same topic, and encourages students to write their own entry by either choosing their own topic or writing about someone they know. Once the week is over, the chart is placed near the word wall, where it becomes a word bank for a daily dictated sentence (described later in this chapter). Students learn to use the word bank to help with spelling, and they continue to use it throughout the year. The chart stays on the word wall for 2 or 3 weeks and is then moved to another area in the classroom. Other charts take its place.

Shirl conducts the same 5-day procedure for each of the other three charts. She introduces the chart, the class brainstorms ideas, students add to their Topics I Can Write About charts, Shirl shares corresponding children's books or poems, and then she models several entries in her treasure book on the related topics.

Transitioning to five-page books. Once these lessons are completed, treasure books then become an independent activity (see Shirl's daily schedule in Table 1-2), and Shirl switches to the five-page book format as described in chapter 2. Her writing workshop transitions into a focus on target skills, VOICES, and writing in other genres.

Writing Instruction in Kindergarten

Writing about kindergartners, Calkins (1986) says that "when we give children the time, materials, and encouragement to write, they use whatever they *do* know in amazing ways" (p. 37). A cursory look at a kindergarten child's writing, however, may make Calkins' assertion difficult to believe. How can scribbles and random letters show amazing things about a child's writing?

When we carefully examine a kindergarten child's writing sample, we can see what it has to teach us about the writer. We can determine what the child knows about letters and words, what he understands about the function of print, and how he uses illustrations to convey a message. If we follow a child's writing over several months, we will be able to determine her growth and development and see all that she is learning. Each child *is* a writer, albeit one at the early stages of writing development.

Most kindergartners fall within the oral message and beginning stages of writing development. Writers in the oral message stage don't yet understand that writing involves words that a reader must interpret. They draw, scribble, write letterlike forms, or write random letters. Writers in the beginning stage of writing development are starting to understand that writing must contain letters and words, but the words are usually not spelled conventionally. These young writers may copy environmental print or use only initial consonants to write their message. Some children in the beginning stage begin to experiment with final consonants and vowel sounds. Instruction for students in these writing stages focuses on developing concepts about letters and words while maintaining attention to content. Chapter 8 contains more information on developmental stages.

Adaptations

Our primary format for young writers, as we discussed in chapter 2, is a five-page book. This format, however, is unlikely to be appropriate for kindergartners because it's doubtful that most children will be able to sustain interest and motivation over the week or more it takes to produce a five-page book. Therefore, adaptations to this format are required for our youngsters in kindergarten. The two adaptations that we've found effective are writing journals and three-page books. The writing journal is the same format as the journal Shirl uses at the beginning of first grade—about 20 sheets of unlined paper stapled into a construction-paper cover. The journal becomes the vehicle for writing at the beginning of kindergarten. As children become more adept at writing, they move into three-page books, an organizational technique similar to five-page books. With a three-page book, however, students concentrate on one page for the beginning, one page for the middle, and the last page for the ending. In addition, other forms of writing are modeled and encouraged.

A Lesson Sequence for Kindergartners

Debbie has worked in Suzy Price's kindergarten class, and together they developed a lesson sequence that has proved to work well for their young writers. They prepare a writing journal for each student and make an enlarged journal for the teacher with 11-by-18-inch white construction paper and a poster-board cover. They begin with a journal format because "it's a great way to note students' achievements and needs, as well as an easy way to launch the writing program" (Routman, 2000, p. 257).

Debbie and Suzy follow the lesson sequence delineated in Table 5-1. The lessons have been discussed elsewhere in this text, and most are simplified versions of Shirl's beginning-of-the-year lessons, described earlier.

A sample of one of Debbie's modeled writings is shown in Figure 5-2. In this sample, Debbie has written, "Mr. Rickards loves to cook." As she wrote this, she thought aloud about selecting a topic, planning the writing, counting the number of words in the sentence, using sound-spelling, consulting the word wall, and ensuring that the picture matches the words.

Figure 5-2. Debbie's Journal Entry

Table 5-1. Lesson Sequence for Beginning Kindergartners

Lesson	Focus
1	• Writers write about people they know.
2	• Writers make a plan before they write (oral rehearsal). • Target skills • Did-it dots
3	• Writers use words and letters when they write.
4	• Writers use turtle talk and the word wall.
5	• Writers write about things they do.
6	• Writers make their words match their pictures.
7	• Writers make words go from left to right.
8	• Writers leave spaces between words.
9	• Writers use a return sweep when needed.
10	• Writers write about places they go.
11	• Writers use periods at the end of their writing.
12	• Writers share their writing with someone else. • Knee-to-knee sharing
13	• Writers use mostly lowercase letters.
14	• Writers use capital letters at the beginning of each sentence.
15	• Writers share their writing in the Author's Chair.
16	• Writers write about things they do.

Supporting Writers in Kindergarten

We've found that modeling alone is insufficient for moving kindergarten students forward in their writing development. We have several support structures that help students to move ahead. We make sure that we provide assorted print resources, utilize a "help page," and use dictation, when appropriate, to support our young writers.

Print resources. A print-rich environment makes available various resources that children can use to facilitate their writing. (This is true for all children, not just kindergartners.) One such print resource is the word wall. Thematic charts are another helpful resource. These are charts that contain words related to a unit of study—winter, insects, or Japan, for example. As a student is writing about a topic that's correlated to a unit the class has studied, the child can consult the chart to help with spelling or to facilitate topic choice. Another helpful resource is an alphabet poster. A poster such as this helps students to think about letters and their sounds as they attempt to turtle-talk. We like the graphics available in *Words Their Way* (Bear et. al, 2000). The authors not only provide posters for initial consonant sounds, they also supply graphics for vowel and consonant blends and digraphs. These posters can be enlarged to the size you need for display, or they can be reduced for individual use. We like to copy the individual poster and tape them to each student's desk or table.

The help page. Utilizing the 'help page' is an idea that Debbie began with kindergarten writers to help extend their knowledge of letter-sound relationships. The *help page* is adapted from an idea used by Reading Recovery™ teachers. She requires students to use the right side of their open journal, leaving the left side for her use (Figure 5-3). On the help page, Debbie records each student's text so that she documents what each child has written. Also, she uses the help page to discuss letters and words with individual students as she moves around the room and confers.

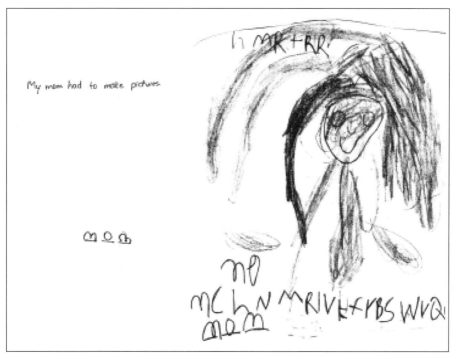

Figure 5-3. Mary's Completed Help Page and Journal Entry

Mary's writing sample in Figure 5-3 provides a good illustration of Debbie's use of the help page. As she knelt by the table, Debbie noticed that Mary used random letters to convey her message. Debbie decided to work with Mary to help her notice that words are made of particular letters. Mary first read her text: My mom had to make pictures. Debbie said, "Mary, I'm going to write your words on this help page so we'll always be able to read them. I'll write your words the way grown-ups write." After writing the sentence conventionally, Debbie decides to work with Mary on the word *mom*. She chooses this word because it's a short, decodable word. Debbie will also be able to link the *m* sound in *mom* to Mary's name. She continues:

> You're writing about your mom, aren't you? Let's use the help page and we'll work together to spell <u>mom</u>. I'm going to turtle-talk the word. M-o-m. I heard three sounds, so I'm going to draw three lines on the help page. Now you turtle-talk the word with me.

Together Mary and Debbie sound out the word *mom*. Then Debbie says, "The word *mom* starts the same as *Mary*. What letter is that?" When Mary replies, Debbie asks her to write an *M* on the first line (see Fig. 5-3). Debbie then continues, "M-o-m. The next sound is O. That's the letter O. I'll write the letter here on the middle line. Now let's figure out the last sound. M-o-m. Yes, we need another M." Mary writes the M on the last line, and Debbie praises her work. "Good job, Mary. You've just written the word *mom*. We used turtle talk to write it. Next time you write about your mom, you'll know how to spell it."

As Debbie moves on to the next student, she notices that Mary copies the word *mom* onto her journal page. Although Mary is not yet ready to sound-spell on her own, Debbie feels confident that she has helped Mary to learn a little bit more about the letter M and the word *mom*.

Dictation. For some kindergarten students who need additional assistance, dictation can be a supportive structure that helps them to move forward. Although we recommend that you use dictation sparingly, when you are the scribe, a struggling student can then focus on creativity and imagination to complete the writing. As Routman (2000) says, "Unburdened by transcription, the child is free to focus on his story or message" (p. 399).

Expanding Beyond Journal Writing

Routman's experiences helped us to realize that journal writing was a necessary but insufficient format for kindergartners. Students need many functional reasons for writing (Calkins, 1986) and will want to move beyond their journals into other modes of writing. Routman (2000) suggests a workable sequence of writing genres for kindergartners: journals, yes-no surveys, lists, letter and card writing, research, poetry, and book reviews. The following list gives some of the many other options for target skills that are appropriate for kindergarten writers:

- ✓ Make a list.
- ✓ Make a label.
- ✓ Write a letter or card.
- ✓ When sharing, read with appropriate volume.
- ✓ When sharing, set a purpose for listening.
- ✓ Tell your partner what you see in your drawing or writing.

- ✓ Tell your partner what you know about your drawing or writing.
- ✓ Use labeled diagrams to explain.
- ✓ Use specific names for people and pets.
- ✓ Give a compliment when you hear another writer using a target skill.
- ✓ Tell or write what happened.
- ✓ Tell or write what is happening.
- ✓ When sharing, tell what your partner wrote.
- ✓ Revise by adding another letter or word to your writing.
- ✓ Add information that tells where something occurred.
- ✓ Ask a question.
- ✓ Make a comparison (-er, -est, simile).
- ✓ Give an opinion (I think…, I know…).
- ✓ Use shape, age, material words.

The planning maps in chapter 3 may also help you to determine target skills for your kindergartners. All target skills should be modeled and supported as students experiment with other modes of writing.

Modifications for Struggling Writers

Struggling writers come in all shapes, sizes, and experience levels. They may have a learning disability, have English as their second language, or simply be behind their peers academically. Regardless of the reason, these students will require modifications in order to reach their potential in writing workshop. Writing workshop is an excellent format for easily accommodating students who are at different levels. The modifications that we suggest don't change the basic structure behind writing workshop; they simply add an extra level of support to help those who are struggling. Many modifications have already been described in this chapter. Because students are different in their instructional needs and learning styles, you'll have to experiment with several ideas to see what works best for each individual. The following list gives our suggested modifications for struggling writers:

- ✓ Capitalize on the power of modeling.
- ✓ Reduce the number of pages required.
- ✓ Use interactive writing.

✓ Use dictation.

✓ Provide an assortment of print resources.

✓ Use a cross-age tutor or parent volunteer as a scribe.

✓ Allow collaboration between peers, with the stronger student serving as the scribe.

✓ Let the struggling student tape-record his or her "writing," then transcribe it.

✓ Utilize a word processing program if handwriting is the issue.

Enriched Word Study

We gave up spelling tests long ago because the effort didn't transfer to children's actual writing. We no longer get our spelling words from a textbook, with students completing a textbook exercise each day. We've found that by utilizing a word wall and giving explicit instruction in words and word patterns, our students have become much better spellers than when we strictly used the basal spelling program. The bonus is that our students are not only learning spelling skills, they are also transferring these skills into their writing.

A word wall is a large bulletin board that's clearly visible to all students. We display the words alphabetically by their first letter. The selection of the words varies from school to school and district to district, but the word wall includes words that students will need often in their reading and writing. We give you a brief summary here, but if you want to know more about word walls and some support activities, see *Phonics They Use* by Patricia Cunningham (1991).

Activities

We'll use Shirl's word study program to illustrate how we help students to understand words and word patterns. Shirl's program utilizes the high-frequency words on the word wall, a phonics board with key words and pictures (Figure 5-4), and theme-related word charts (Figure 5-5). For example, *what* is a high-frequency word on the word wall; *boat* is the key word for the *oa* chunk and is on the phonics board; and seasonal words, such as *flowers, rain, rainbow, butterfly,* and *caterpillar,* are on a chart labeled "Spring." (Shirl uses Microsoft® Greetings Workshop software for illustrations on her phonics board.)

Each week, Shirl adds five new words to the word wall and one key word (with a corresponding picture) to the phonics board. Themed word charts are brainstormed by the students and completed as needed during social studies or science time. After introducing the words, Shirl has a routine that she completes every day with her first graders. Students number their paper 1 through 19. Then Shirl dictates words that students write by using the word wall, phonics board, and themed word charts to spell the dictated words. As students write, Shirl moves throughout the room, providing support as needed. (During the first six weeks of school, students number their papers 1–11. They work with five word-wall words, five words related to a phonics principle, and one dictated sentence.)

Figure 5-4. Phonics Board

<u>Spring</u>

flowers	kite	rainbow
bloom	wind	cloud
sun	bird	bluebonnet
baby	rain	butterfly
cool	egg	caterpillar
nest	rabbit	vacation

Figure 5-5. Themed Word Chart

We'll use Mike's sample in Figure 5-6 and Shirl's oral directions to illustrate. For numbers 1 through 5, Shirl studies her students' written work to determine high-frequency words that need review. In this instance, she dictates the following:

1. Write the word *or*. Do you want juice or milk?

2. Write the word *when*. When are we going to lunch?

3. Write the word *one*. I have one new shirt.

4. Write the word *have*. Do you have a pencil I can use?

5. Write the word *what*. What are you doing?

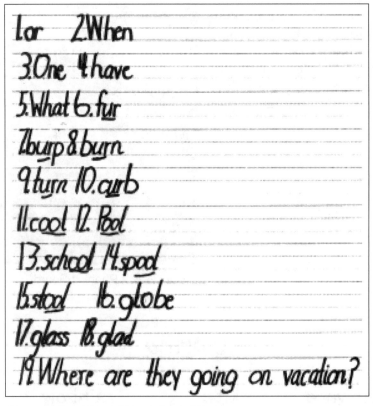

Figure 5-6.   Mike's Word Study Work

The next segment focuses on the new phonics element. In this case, Shirl has just introduced *ur*. On the phonics board, she displays the key word *purse* with an accompanying illustration. The *ur* in *purse* is printed in a contrasting color to the rest of the word. Shirl dictates as follows:

6. Use the key word *purse* to spell *fur*. The bear has brown fur.

7. Use the key word *purse* to spell *burp*. The root beer made me burp.

8. Use the key word *purse* to spell *burn.* Don't burn yourself on the hot oven.

9. Use the key word *purse* to spell *turn.* It's my turn to roll the dice.

10. Use the key word *purse* to spell *curb.* He parked the car beside the curb.

The next five words relate to a word family. Shirl chooses the family *ool* for review. This chunk is selected from a list of high-frequency word families. Shirl continues by pointing to the key word *moon* on the phonics board.

11. Use the word *moon* to spell *cool.* It was cool outside last night.

12. Use the word *cool* to spell *pool.* I wish I had a pool in my backyard.

13. Use the word *pool* to spell *school.* I love to go to school.

14. Use the word *school* to spell *spool.* I used the spool of white thread.

15. Use the word *spool* to spell *stool.* Jay climbed up on the stool.

The next three words review some phonics or language element that the class has studied previously. Sometimes Shirl uses this segment to practice endings, plurals, contractions, compound words, prefixes, or suffixes. In this instance, she asks her students to utilize a previously studied phonics element – the consonant blend *gl.*

16. Use the key word *glasses* to spell *globe.* I found Africa on our globe.

17. Use the key word *glasses* to spell *glass.* Oops! I broke the glass.

18. Use the key word *glasses* to spell *glad.* I am glad you're in my room.

Shirl's final daily task is for the students to write a sentence that she dictates. The sentence will include words from the word wall, words that the students will have to spell using a phonics pattern, and words from the theme chart. For this lesson, Shirl wants her students to use the spring theme chart in this dictation. She also wants her students to practice using a question mark appropriately.

19. Where are they going on vacation?

Shirl has found that the dictation sentence works best if she reads the sentence word by word. She doesn't say the whole sentence until every word has been dictated. She reminds students to put a space after every word in the sentence.

After she dictates each word and students have finished writing it, Shirl calls on a student to spell the word while she writes it on a chart. When they've completed all 19 words, they read the chart out loud together.

This word study session takes about 15 minutes each day, with a few more minutes needed on Monday to introduce the new word-wall words and phonics element. This isn't the only time Shirl's students work with words, however. Word study is also done during guided reading, interactive writing, and writing workshop.

Chapter

Using Nonfiction to Link Reading and Writing

For students to write well in this genre, we also need to show them how the writer makes the topic appealing through engaging writing, clear and inviting visual aids, and logical organization.

—Regie Routman, *Conversations*

Think about your actions when you picked up this book for the first time. You probably read the title first and then turned to the back cover to read the summary. Then you might have examined the table of contents to see if the information in this book interested you. Maybe you turned to a particular chapter and read the headings and studied some tables and figures. Perhaps the books in our reference list piqued your interest. You might have read the information about the authors to make sure that we were credible writers on the topic of primary writing. You probably made connections to your own instructional practices or asked questions about some aspect of writing. All of those habits describe what good readers do when they first encounter a nonfiction text. This chapter will focus on developing the habits of good nonfiction readers in our young students, and then using this knowledge to research a topic and write a nonfiction piece.

Why Nonfiction?

Nonfiction is obviously different from fiction. Nonfiction texts are factual and often combine the written word with graphics. There are different forms and purposes attached to nonfiction than to fiction. In the past, teachers have concentrated their instruction on fiction, but we've come to see the importance of balancing our attention between fiction and nonfiction. The principal reason for an emphasis on nonfiction is that 85% of the reading done by students once they enter middle school is nonfiction (Snowball, 1995). In addition, nonfiction helps students to increase their knowledge, make connections, observe, question, and investigate (Routman, 2000). In order to prepare students for this kind of reading, it's imperative that we teach students about nonfiction in the early grades.

Immersion in Reading

Routman states:

> Before we can expect students to read and write nonfiction competently on their own, they must be given the opportunity to listen to it being read aloud, discuss its attributes, observe as the techniques of demonstrating it are modeled, and browse through a wide range of informational material. Our students need to be aware of the purposes for reading nonfiction and of how and why these books are researched, written, and organized." (p. 443)

Although our book addresses writing instruction, many nonfiction read-aloud opportunities *must* precede writing.

   In addition to using nonfiction books during guided reading, Shirl has found a read-aloud routine for nonfiction that works well for her. She reads nonfiction daily, either from a big book or a little book, but she reads only a little bit at a time. This has several advantages. First, it's quick, and time is a precious commodity. Second, it builds background knowledge to help students gain a deeper understanding of the topic being studied. For example, if Shirl reads a nonfiction book about weather all in one day, her students have a big content load to hear and understand very quickly. They hear information about clouds, precipitation, the water cycle, storms, weather instruments, and so on, and they can't begin to understand and remember all of this information in one sitting. Instead, Shirl might model browsing through the book one day, reading and thinking aloud about the table of contents the next day, reading a section on clouds the third day, studying a diagram about the water cycle the next day, and so on. In this way, students are better able to understand, retain the information, and make connections between new information and prior knowledge. A third advantage of Shirl's nonfiction read-aloud routine is that it allows her to continually model, think aloud, and discuss the unique features of nonfiction.

Features of Nonfiction

Nonfiction includes both informational and biographical texts. It includes reading from manuals, brochures, textbooks, newspapers, pamphlets, the Internet, and catalogs. In addition to reading the words, readers of nonfiction must attend to the graphic elements of nonfiction such as captions, diagrams, maps, and time lines. The skill of interpreting these elements is called *visual literacy.* Moline (1995) asserts:

> Information literacy is more than communicating with words, because many informational texts also include important visual elements, such as diagrams, graphs, maps and tables. . . . Students of all ages encounter these visual texts as frequently as adults do and are expected to understand them, both in school work and in everyday living. To reflect this range of literacies, a classroom program needs to include explicit instruction in how these texts work. (p. 1)

In addition, nonfiction books are organizationed in a way that makes it easier for the reader to understand the information. In first and second grades, students should be familiarized with these text features and text structures to help them better understand the information presented in a nonfiction book.

Text Features

Not only must we teach the pictorial features of nonfiction such as captions, labeled diagrams, and graphs, we must also help children to learn about the print features of nonfiction such as the table of contents, the glossary, headings, and boldface words. Table 6-1 illustrates some of the nonfiction text features that are appropriate for primary readers and writers. It's our responsibility as primary teachers to help students learn about these nonfiction features so that they will be prepared for the social studies, science, and math texts that they'll encounter in the intermediate grades. In addition, visual literacy is a life skill that we need in order to function in our everyday lives (Moline, 1995).

We share here one way to introduce some of these nonfiction text features to primary students. Of course, kindergarten teachers would introduce fewer fea-

Table 6-1. Nonfiction Text Features

Visual Features	Print Features
bar graph	highlighted text
line graph	boldface type
photograph	italics
picture with caption	headings
time line	table of contents
simple map	index
labeled diagram	glossary
simple table	white space to separate items
cross-section	large and small type
scaled diagram	
web	

tures than would first-grade teachers. Second-grade teachers may only have to review the features if students learned them in first grade. You'll need to do some preassessment in order to determine which features to highlight. Before the first lesson, you should collect some nonfiction books (preferably big books), or you could use a social studies or science textbook. It's helpful if you have a book that corresponds to the social studies or science unit your class is working on, to allow you to conduct this lesson sequence during your content area time.

Shirl began this format in her first-grade class after hearing Brenda Parkes speak at an early literacy conference. Subsequently, Shirl read *Read It Again!* by Parkes (2000), in which this format was explained further. Based upon Parkes's ideas, the following bulleted list describes a sequence of steps you can use to introduce nonfiction text features. We purposefully haven't described a day-by-day plan. You'll be able to adjust the lessons to your time schedule and combine some of the ideas into a single lesson. Our explanations give directions for use with a big book; you'll need to make some slight adaptations if you're using a textbook.

- To introduce the table of contents, say, "Look at the title of the book. If you were writing about _____, what information would you want the reader to learn? What do you already know about ___?" Record student responses. Then work together to categorize the responses into related groups. Point to the table of contents page. Say, "Do you know what this page is called? Why do you think the author put a page like this in the book?" Read the contents page and compare with the categories chosen by the students. Use the table of contents to decide where to start reading, based upon the interest of your students. Point out that you don't have to start at the beginning in a nonfiction book.

- To discuss its attributes, open to the table of contents. Ask, "What do you notice about the print on this page? What did the author do to make the contents page?" If students don't notice, point out the different sizes of print, capital letters in each heading, numbers to show page locations, and so on. Each time you introduce a new nonfiction book, use the contents to locate specific information (e.g., on what page would we find out what bears eat?). If you find a nonfiction book without a table of contents, you and your students can work together to create one.

- Open to a double-page spread. Ask, "How does the author present information on these two pages?" Help students to identify pictures, photos, and words rather than specific content. Read the text and discuss the pictures. Then discuss first what they learned by listening to the words and then what they learned by looking at the pictures.

- Before this lesson, use paper to cover the pictures on another double-page spread. Read the text. Discuss and record what the students learned from listening to the words. Remove the paper from the pictures. Ask, "What new information do we have now? What can we learn from the pictures? How does the picture help us to understand the words?" Discuss and record the new information obtained from the pictures.

- Open to another double-page spread. "Read" the pictures first. Ask "What do we know by reading the pictures?" Then read the text and again discuss how the pictures helped with understanding.

- Using another double-page spread, point to the heading. Ask "Where have we seen these words before?" Guide students to recall that they'd seen the words in the table of contents. Say "This is called the heading. Where is the heading located on the page? How are these words different from the words on the rest of the page?" Usually the words are bigger, in boldface print, in color, or highlighted. Continue with "Why did the author put a heading on this page? What does it tell us? How does it help us?" Read the section to the students. Conclude that a heading tells us the main idea or what the passage is about.

- Open to another double-page spread. Read the heading. Ask "What do you think we'll learn in this section?"

- Cover up the heading on a double-page spread. Read the section. Ask "What would be a good heading for this section? How would we write it so that the reader will know it's a heading?" Uncover the heading and discuss.

- Select a nonfiction book that doesn't have section headings. Show several pages to the students. Ask "Do all nonfiction books have headings?" Work together to write several headings for the book.

- Read the title of a new nonfiction book. Ask students to predict what headings they'll find in the table of contents. Read the contents to confirm or refute their predictions.

- Preview the new book by quickly flipping through and reading the headings. Then turn to a page with a picture that has a caption. Read the section, then read the caption and discuss its attributes. Ask "Where is the caption located? How are these words different from the rest of the text?" The caption's text usually has smaller print and short sentences, phrases, or word labels. Continue discussing these questions: Why did the author add a caption here? How do they help the reader? Do the captions contain new information or do they repeat information from the text?

- Turn to another double-page spread that includes captions. Locate and read the heading. Ask "What will you probably learn about on these two pages?" Locate and read the captions. Ask what the students learned by reading the pictures and captions. Read the text. Ask "Did the captions contain new or repeated information from the main text?"

- Show a page with a picture that doesn't have a caption. Ask "Do all pictures in nonfiction books have captions?" Read the heading and text, then discuss the picture. Work together to compose an appropriate caption for it. To review the appearance of a caption, ask "How do we need to write these words so that the reader will know they are captions?"

- Find a page that includes a labeled diagram. Read the heading and the text. Share the labels on the diagram and lead the students in determining that a labeled diagram is a drawing or photograph with each part labeled in small print, with usually only single words or short phrases. Discuss "Why did the author use a labeled diagram? How does it help the reader?"

- Turn to a page where the drawing or photograph is not labeled. After reading and discussing the features, use stick-on notes to label parts included in the picture.

- Find another page where the picture is not labeled. After reading and discussing the features of the section, have students independently draw the picture and label several parts. (Students can also draw and label diagrams for social studies and science throughout the year.)

- Begin a chart similar to the one shown in Table 6-2. Review the features you've already studied and glue a photocopied example of each feature. Have your students help you to determine the purpose of each feature. Whenever you introduce a new nonfiction feature, add more information to the chart.

- Show students an index. Ask "Why did the author put an index in this book? How does it help the reader?" Discuss the attributes of an index (its location in the back of a book, lowercase print, usually single words or short phrases followed by a comma and a page number, and alphabetical order). Show how to use an index to locate specific information.

- Each time you start a new book, use the contents and the index prior to reading the text so that you can locate specific information. Model how to scan the text and pictures to locate information quickly.

- Construct an index by working together to alphabetize content vocabulary following a social studies, science, or math unit.

- Introduce a glossary. Discuss its attributes (location in the back of the book, alphabetical order, key word in bold print, comma, pronunciation guide in parentheses, colon, definition). Ask "Why did the author put a glossary in this book? How does it help the reader?"

- Being able to define a word requires extensive oral vocabulary building. Practice defining even very simple words, like *fish*, while reading nonfiction books together.

- Work together to create a short glossary for a nonfiction book that doesn't include one.

- Help students to write glossaries for social studies, science, or math units.

- As the year progresses, highlight other visual and print features of nonfiction texts (see Table 6-1).

- Use Wikki-Stix™ or highlighter tape to emphasize vocabulary common in nonfiction: (a) words showing passage of time, (b) words showing quantity, (c) descriptive words, (d) similes, and (e) words showing comparison.

- Model how to scan for definitions of vocabulary words within the text.

Table 6-2.   Nonfiction Features Chart

Features of Nonfiction				
Feature	Table of Contents	Heading	Caption	Labeled Diagram
Example	(picture)	(picture)	(picture)	(picture)
Purpose				

As we work extensively with nonfiction text features in read-alouds and the content areas, we also work on text structures. The next section gives information about developing an awareness of text structures in our primary students.

Text Structures

Nonfiction text structures (Vacca & Vacca, 1999) include description, sequence, comparison and contrast, cause and effect, problem and solution, and question and answer. To introduce a nonfiction text structure, we find nonfiction books that are examples of that particular structure in big and small books. We show students how the author has organized the information into one of the text structures. We also include a simple graphic that functions as a visual aid for each text structure to help students identify the organization of a particular book.

Description. In nonfiction books organized by description, the author presents ideas by listing the important characteristics or attributes of the topic. Figure 6-1 contains a graphic for the descriptive text structure.

Sequence. In books with a sequential text structure, the facts, events, or concepts are organized in a sequence. The author either traces the development of the topic or gives the steps in a sequence. Figure 6-2 contains a graphic for the sequential text structure.

Comparison and contrast. Comparison-and-contrast books point out similarities (comparisons) and differences (contrasts) among facts,

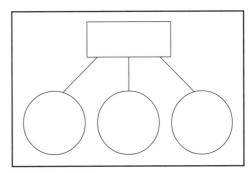

Figure 6-1.   Descriptive Text Structure

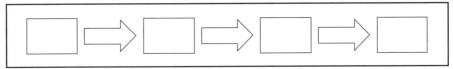

Figure 6-2.   Sequential Text Structure

people, events, concepts, and so on. Figure 6-3 contains a graphic for the comparison-and-contrast text structure.

Cause and effect. These books show how facts, events, or concepts (effects) occur because of other facts, events, or concepts (causes). Figure 6-4 contains a graphic for the cause-and-effect text structure.

Problem and solution. Problem-and-solution books show the development of a problem, then delineate possible solutions. Figure 6-5 contains a graphic for the problem-and-solution text structure.

Question and answer. Question-and-answer books pose questions related to a particular topic and then answer each question. The problem-and-solution graphic (see Fig. 6-5) is also appropriate as a graphic for question-and-answer text structures.

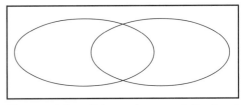

Figure 6-3.   Comparison-and-Contrast Text Structure

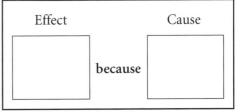

Figure 6-4.   Cause-and-Effect Text Structure

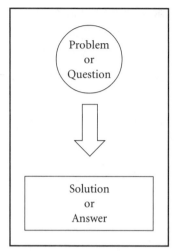

Figure 6-5.   Problem-and-Solution and Question-and-Answer Text Structures

Writing Opportunities

As we've said, we want to make certain that our children have a thorough understanding of the structures and features that make up nonfiction texts. They hear nonfiction read aloud, and they read nonfiction themselves when they are participating in guided reading, literacy stations, and independent reading.

Using Text Features in Writing

After students have had some experience reading nonfiction books, they can begin to apply their knowledge of text features in short writing lessons. The feature you choose for them to do depends on the task and content area on which you're working. For example, when completing a unit on butterflies in science, Shirl's first graders made labeled diagrams of a caterpillar. They also made a glossary of three words related to butterflies to share with their parents. After a field trip, Shirl's class made time lines showing the things they had done during the trip. Some other suggestions for short writing lessons to integrate into math, science, or social studies include the following:

✓ Writing captions for pictures they've drawn

✓ Writing captions for photographs of class activities

✓ Finding the most important word in their learning log entry and making it boldface

✓ Making a heading for a learning log entry

✓ Drawing a labeled diagram

- ✓ Making a time line
- ✓ Writing a glossary of vocabulary words, with pronunciation guide, related to a unit of study
- ✓ Writing an index for a nonfiction book that doesn't have one
- ✓ Writing a short paragraph using one of the nonfiction text structures

Of course, you will model these activities first and provide plenty of support and guidance while they're learning to write these features of nonfiction.

Writing Nonfiction Books

After many various experiences with nonfiction, our students are now ready to write a full book on one topic. Just as we did in chapter 2, where we introduced five-page books in Debbie's classroom, we'll use Shirl's room as her first graders begin a unit in April on animals and their special characteristics.

The first step in making nonfiction books is to decide on the unit of study. Shirl decides that she wants her students to research animals. She knows that this will be a motivating topic and that she has plenty of books available that cover a wide range of animals. She finds books in her private collection, in the school library, and at her local public library. Shirl learned an important lesson from a mistake she made the first year she tried this sequence of lessons. She first let her students pick the kinds of animal they wanted to study, and then she had to scramble to find appropriate primary-level books for them to use. Now she gathers sets of nonfiction titles, two or three books on each animal, and puts the sets into plastic zip-lock bags so she can pass them out easily. Shirl shows her students a brief preview of all the sets, then she asks them to write down their top three animal choices. She uses those three choices to determine partners (two students work together to do their research) and an appropriate animal for each pair. She's learned to give more familiar animals to her at-risk students who need more support and who mostly gather information from the photographs. She makes a chart with the names of the student partners and their research topics and displays this in her classroom. She also gathers nonfiction big books to serve as models for the features she wants to address. (If big books are not available to you, you can photocopy pages with the different nonfiction features and display them on the overhead projector.)

Just as we do with our five-page books, Shirl prepares a set of books for her students, plus one for herself. These books will look a little different from the five-page books described in chapter 2. Shirl copies three pages per student of fully lined paper. One sheet serves as the first page of the nonfiction book; students will use it to write the table of contents. Two other fully lined sheets are placed at the end, serving as pages for glossary and index. The middle pages are half-lined sheets. The number of middle sheets depends on the number of headings you want your students to write. Shirl decides that she wants her first grad-ers to include four headings. Thus her books are made up of seven pages: one fully lined page, four half-lined pages, and two fully lined pages. She makes extra fully lined sheets in case students need to add pages when they have more information under each heading than will fit on one half-lined sheet.

Lesson 1: Introduction

On the first day of this nonfiction writing unit, Shirl tells her students:

> We've been studying a lot about nonfiction. We've learned about the purpose of nonfiction—to give information. We've learned that a nonfiction book has features such as a table of contents, headings, captions, and an index. What other fea-tures have we learned about?

After students respond, Shirl continues, "We're going to start writing our own nonfiction books, and we're going to study animals. Here are the books we'll use." Shirl shares the book sets she's gathered, and then the students choose their top three choices as described above. This lesson doesn't take the full 35–40 minutes that Shirl schedules for writing workshop, so she directs the stu-dents to return to the five-page book on which they'd been working. This will be a routine that occurs daily; students go back to their five-page books after completing the nonfiction task.

Lesson 2: Target Skill—Write a Table of Contents

First Shirl presents the chart that she's made displaying the partners and topics for research. Then she resumes by saying, "Today we're going to start writing our own nonfiction books. What features could we include?" Students review nonfiction features. Shirl then asks, "What will our readers want to learn about each animal?" She makes a list as students respond with ideas such as where the animal lives, what it looks like, how it protects itself, what its enemies are, and so on. Next the students vote on the four headings they'd like to have in their books. They decide to in-clude the animal's appearance, its habitat, its diet, and how it pro-tects itself.

Shirl now turns to the big book and displays the table of contents. She asks students what they ob-serve about it. They notice that the

Table of Contents.
What It Looks Like
Where It Lives
What It Eats
Protection
Glossary
Index

Figure 6-6. Anna's Table of Contents

headings are capitalized like titles, and they observe that there are dots that separate the heading from the page number. Shirl passes out the books she's constructed and asks the students to open to the first page. Shirl models the table of contents in her book while students write in theirs. Together they construct the table of contents, including the chapter headings, glossary, and index. They realize they must omit the page numbers until their books are completed. Figure 6-6 shows Anna's table of contents.

Lesson 3: Target Skill—Read and Restate

Shirl reviews the chart with the partners and the animal about which each pair will be writing. Then she says, "My book will be about millipedes. How could I find information on what a millipede looks like?" Students suggest looking at the table of contents, studying the index, examining the photographs, and skimming the text for key words—all methods for locating information that they had practiced during their daily shared reading of nonfiction. She locates information on a millipede's appearance and reads it aloud to the class. She then covers the text and restates the information in her own words.

Next, partners are given their bag of books and directed to find out all they can about the appearance of their animal. Shirl sets her timer for 10 minutes. She's found that she needs to control the time they spend researching, or some students will read quickly and move to another task before they have done a thorough job of reading. Ten minutes is an arbitrary amount of time; Shirl monitors her students to see if more time is needed. She reminds them to say the information in their own words because they will not be able to copy from the books. She monitors and supports as partners share the information they are learning.

After 10 minutes have passed and the books have been put away, Shirl models recalling the information about a millipede's appearance, writing the heading, skipping a line, and then writing the information in her own words. Students (alone, not with the partner) write their heading and information about the appearance of their animal. When finished, they use a black marker to outline their heading. If students need more than one page to write about what their animal looks like, Shirl helps them to remove the staples from their books and insert an extra page.

Figure 6-7 shows Anna's text under the heading "What It Looks Like." It says, "Guinea pigs have 2 big eyes and 2 ears. They have no tail. Some guinea pigs are white, black, brown, and all colors on one guinea pig. They have one nose and one mouth. And they have 4 sharp claws."

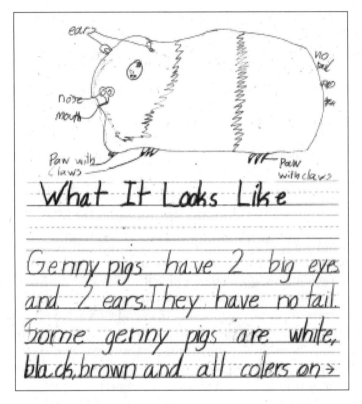

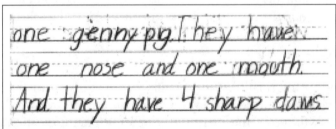

Figure 6-7. Anna's Text and Labeled Diagram About a Guinea Pig's Appearance

Lesson 4: Target Skill—Make a Labeled Diagram

Using a nonfiction big book, Shirl and her students review the attributes of a labeled diagram. (An alternative to making a labeled diagram is to have students make a scaled drawing showing the relative size of their animal compared to a familiar object.) Shirl models by using a photograph to draw a millipede in the space above the first heading. She reminds the students to label each part, using the book to help with spelling. She allows students to use books from their animal set so that their drawings will be more scientific. Finally, students draw and label their diagram. In Figure 6-7, Anna's labels are *ears, nose, mouth, paws with claws,* and *no tail.*

Lesson 5: Second Heading—Habitat

Shirl follows the same procedures as in Lesson 2, focusing on each animal's habitat. Shirl locates information about a millipede's habitat, reads orally, closes the book, and then restates in her own words. Students then get together with their partners and spend 10 minutes using the words or illustrations to locate information and restate in their own words. Shirl models recording the heading and habitat information and the children record their own heading and information, and then outline the heading. Anna's text in Figure 6-8 says, "Guinea pigs live in a cage because they are a pet. In the cage they have a place that separates the eating room and the sleeping room. They do not like the hot. They like to be in the shade."

Lesson 6: Target Skill— Write a Caption

Using a nonfiction big book, the students review the attributes and purpose of captions. (An alternative is to make a cross-section drawing of an animal's habitat.) Shirl again looks at a photograph of a millipede to draw her illustration. She then summarizes information about a millipede's habitat into a caption and writes the caption in small letters beneath her illustration. Students complete the same task using their book, and Shirl models and supports as needed. In Figure 6-8, Anna has drawn a guinea pig's cage. Her caption reads, "Guinea pigs live in a cage." She has also labeled the parts of her illustration with *food, water bottle, tunnel,* and *sleeping room.*

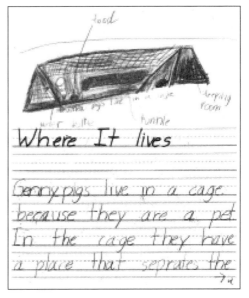

Figure 6-8. Anna's Text and Illustration With Caption About a Guinea Pig's Habitat

Lesson 7: Third Heading—Diet

Shirl follows the same procedures as in Lesson 2 but this time focuses on each animal's diet. Shirl locates appropriate information and reads it aloud, then closes the book and restates it in her own words. Students then locate information about what their animal eats (in the text or the pictures) and restate the information. Shirl and her students write the information on the next page of their book, outlining the heading. In Figure 6-9, Anna's text reads, "The guinea pigs eat hay, grain, green grass, drinks clean water, carrots, cabbage leaves, and cucumbers."

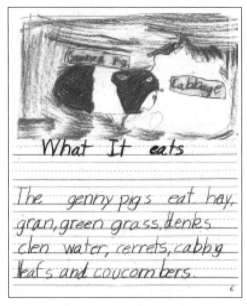

Figure 6-9.   Anna's Text About a Guinea Pig's Diet

Lesson 8: Target Skill—Use Highlighted Labels

Using a nonfiction book, Shirl and her students first review the attributes and purpose of a highlighted label. To model her illustration, Shirl uses a photograph of a millipede eating. Then she writes the word *millipede,* draws a box around the word, and colors inside the box with a yellow marker. She does the same thing with the word *lettuce.* Next, students use their books to locate a picture of their animal eating. They also draw a picture, write the name of their animal and its food, draw a box around the label, and color the box yellow. In Anna's illustration in Figure 6-9, she has highlighted the words *guinea pig* and *cabbage.*

Lesson 9: Fourth Heading—Protection

Shirl again follows the same procedures as in Lesson 2, reading and thinking out loud about the information related to how millipedes protect themselves. Students then use the text or pictures in their books to locate the information and restate it in their own words. Next, Shirl models in her book, and students write their information and outline the headings. In Figure 6-10, Anna wrote, "A guinea pig lives in a cage so the dogs and cat cannot get it. Guinea pigs do not like the sun, so if they are in the sun, they go into their napping box in their cage."

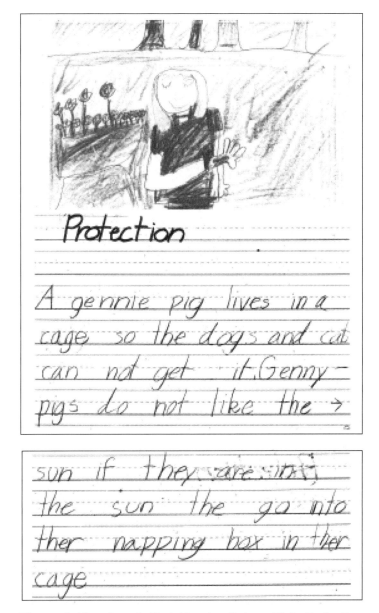

Figure 6-10. Anna's Text About a Guinea Pig's Protection

Lesson 10: Picture

Shirl uses a photograph of a millipede curled up in a tight spiral to show how it protects itself. She illustrates her picture and then decides to add a caption. Students use their book sets to locate a picture showing their animals' defense mechanisms. They illustrate their text and add a caption if desired. Figure 6-10 shows Anna's picture of a guinea pig being protected by its owner.

Lesson 11: Target Skill—Write a Glossary

Using a nonfiction book, Shirl and her students review the attributes of a glossary. Shirl models the construction of a glossary using the book she's written about millipedes and three stick-on notes. She says, "I am going to find two or three words that the reader might need help in understanding. As I find each word, I will write it on a stick-on note." Shirl models by writing three words from her millipede book. She then turns to her glossary page and manipulates the three stick-on notes so that they are in alphabetical order. After writing *Glossary* on the first line, she writes the first word to define, then models the pronunciation guide by sound spelling and enclosing in parentheses. (For many students, the spelling of the word and the pronunciation guide will be identical.) The colon comes next, and then Shirl asks her students to help her write a definition. As she writes and defines her second and third words, she asks her students to help her by telling her what to do next. In this way, Shirl checks their understanding.

Shirl provides much support as students select two or three important words from their animal books, write them on stick-on notes, and work on their glossary. Anna's glossary is shown in Figure 6-11. For students who struggle with reading or writing, Shirl will often obtain a few helpers in an upper grade to serve as "assistants."

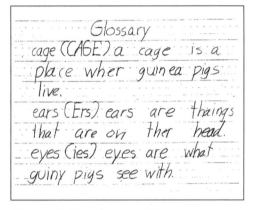

Figure 6-11. Anna's Glossary

Lesson 12: Number Pages, Update Table of Contents

Using her book as a model, Shirl demonstrates how to number the pages. She places the numbers at the bottom of each page. She then models how to match the table of contents heading with the page heading, add the page numbers to the table of contents, and then add dots to match the heading to the page number. Shirl helps students as they complete the task. Anna's updated table of contents page is shown in Figure 6-12.

Table of Contents	1
What It Looks Like	2
Where It Lives	4
What It Eats	6
Protection	8
Glossary	10
Index	11

Figure 6-12. Anna's Completed Table of Contents

Lesson 13: Target Skill—Write an Index

Using the model nonfiction book, the students review the attributes of an index. Shirl then uses another nonfiction book with minimal text and reads a page. The students decide on an important word on the page, and then Shirl flips to the index to see if the word was included. The students quickly observe that most of the time the words they've selected are in the index.

Next, Shirl uses her own nonfiction book to model how to select one important word under each heading, for a total of four words. On four stick-on notes, she writes each word and its page number. Then Shirl turns to her last page and writes the word *Index*, outlining the heading. She arranges her four words in alphabetical order on the blank page adjacent to the index. Finally, she shows students how to write the word, place a comma, and then write the page number. Anna's index is seen in Figure 6-13.

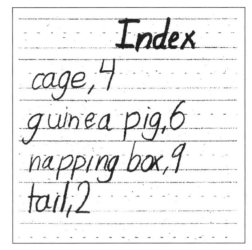

Figure 6-13. Anna's Index

Lesson 14: Cover

Shirl displays several nonfiction books, and the students discuss each book's title and cover picture. They notice that the title is factual and the cover picture is either a photograph or a realistic illustration. Shirl names her own book *Millipedes* and draws a realistic picture of a millipede. Students then complete their cover layout with illustration, title, and author's name.

Lesson 15: Finishing the Book

Students are familiar with the process of including a copyright date, publishing location, and a section about the author. Shirl models with her book, and then students complete their nonfiction book.

Alternatives

The example we've included here demonstrates Shirl's nonfiction writing lessons. Shirl chose the topic of animals because she knew it would be motivating.

You, of course, should select topics that are of interest to your students and correspond with your grade-level curriculum.

Alternative topics that might be suitable for your primary curriculum include writing nonfiction books about famous Americans, inventors, insects, dinosaurs, a continent, a country, or rainforest plants. Before deciding on a topic, you must first make sure that you have enough nonfiction books at an appropriate reading level so that your students can complete their research.

You may also want your students to have other nonfiction writing opportunities that are different from the arrangement Shirl used. Instead of using books to conduct research about an animal, you could do research through direct observation. By using a class pet, like a hamster or a goldfish, students could observe and then complete a class book with headings similar to Shirl's. Another alternative to books is to use Internet sources, but you'll have to screen the information to ensure that it's at an appropriate reading level. If you teach kindergartners, you could pair them with a class of older students and have them complete the research together, or kindergartners could record their information through illustrations only. Students would conduct their research either by direct observation or by using pictorial information in nonfiction books. The important point of any nonfiction writing activity is for students to understand that nonfiction is factual, has special features, and is useful for finding information.

Chapter

7

Opportunities
for Response

Writing is a social act.

—Donald Graves, *A Fresh Look at Writing*

Words are powerful. "Debbie, this worked great! I think you should write a book about it!" Debbie's colleague, Ron Robinson, said this to her after he had tried five-page books with his fourth graders. Ron didn't know the power of the words he had uttered, but Debbie pondered them for months. She then called up Shirl and suggested that they collaborate on a product that ultimately resulted in this book.

Ron's words were compelling. They inspired Debbie to an action that deeply affected her professional life. Similarly, words can powerfully influence our young writers. It's our job to facilitate the conversations in our classrooms so that students gain the language they need to help each other, and so that our language affects the children's writing in positive ways. As Ralph Fletcher (1993) wrote, "We must speak to our students with an honesty tempered by compassion. Our words will literally define the ways they perceive themselves as writers" (p. 19).

The Importance of Social Interaction

When we were in school 30 or more years ago, there weren't many opportunities to write. However, when we did receive a writing assignment, teachers expected it to be a solitary task. Silence was the norm. Feedback from the teacher was almost always in writing and was almost always corrective rather than complimentary. Papers were filled with red marks. *Awkward, run-on,* and *needs transition* were some of the typical phrases we received on our papers. Instruction focused on grammar rather than craft. It's amazing that we learned anything about writing!

Fortunately for students today, teachers now know much more about the conditions that are necessary for effective writing. We know that writers need to talk with others throughout the writing process as they craft a piece. We know that responses from their peers and the teacher help them to discover what they do or do not understand, what they have and have not tried, and what they are or are not communicating in their writing.

Johnson (1999) shares several important functions of social interaction for young writers. First, social interaction reinforces the relationship between written and spoken language. Young writers then understand that what they say and think can be written on paper. This understanding helps students to see how written language can function in everyday settings. Second, social interaction teaches writers an awareness of an audience. As they arrive at this awareness, young writers want the audience to like what they have written, thus increasing their motivation to write effectively. They begin to understand their audience's interests, understandings, and expectations. In addition, interacting with others helps students to reflect on what they've written, which is a necessary step for revision. Freeman (1998) says, "The objective of this writing process stage, *response,* is for young writers to hear their own writing and to realize they have an audience for it. This realization will lead to a conscious consideration for their readers as they mature as writers" (p. 42).

In our classrooms, we have several structures that support our young writers' need to interact with others. We devise opportunities for our students to share with one another, get feedback from each other and from us, and reflect upon their writing based upon their interaction with others.

Response Opportunities

Sharing their work with others provides young writers with the opportunity to rehearse their pieces and celebrate the many successes. The teacher has the chance to reinforce each child's writing attempts and to teach new writing skills and strategies. Response opportunities can happen during the Author's Chair or during several other more informal arrangements. We've found that a balance between formal and informal response opportunities works best in our primary classrooms.

Author's Chair

Author's Chair has become a ritual in many classrooms where writing workshop is conducted. The first essential ingredient to a successful Author's Chair routine is, naturally, a chair with space around it where students can congregate. It can be a special chair that's used only for the Author's Chair routine or a multipurpose chair that serves as a place for class gatherings. For the Author's Chair in her classroom, our friend Dawn Westfall used a director's chair. When she attended professional conferences or bookstore autograph sessions, she'd bring along one of the canvas sections from the chair and ask authors to autograph the material. This became a unique Author's Chair—autographed by published authors and for use by young authors. The Author's Chair in Cindy Cecil's second-grade classroom consists of a bar stool and a special lamp used to shine on the student author. Cindy calls this her "Author Spotlight."

Purposes of the Author's Chair

During an Author's Chair session, one or more writers share their writing with a large group. Then each author invites responses from his or her classmates and the teacher. Graves (1994) lists four purposes of this type of large group format:

- ✓ Young children need to see the effect of their writing on their classmates' faces.

- ✓ Children in the audience need practice in listening and repeating the texts of readers. In this way they gain experience in maintaining an understanding of the parts and whole of a piece.

- ✓ Authors need to find out what their classmates understand and do not understand in each writer's piece.

- ✓ Authors need to experience the joy of everyone's participation in a well-read text.

Although Author's Chair is a place for students to celebrate their writing, it is also a platform for sharing learning experiences. Students can relate information about skills or strategies that they tried, what did or didn't work, new words or target skills they've included, new genres they've tried, and so on. Thus the students not only listen and respond to a classmate's written product, they also benefit from hearing some of the thinking processes that their friends have experienced as they've crafted a piece. Graves gives an additional advantage of sharing through Author's Chair. He writes, "When you help children to share in large group format you also help them to learn the basic elements that will help them share in small groups without the teacher present" (p. 146).

Initiating Author's Chair

Unless your students have already had many successful experiences with Author's Chair, you'll need to set some precedents. We begin the Author's Chair early in the writing process, but we generally wait a few weeks so that we can better establish the other elements of our writing workshop routine. During the first lessons of Author's Chair, we want to teach our students who are reading their pieces how to tell a little something about their writing process and to set a purpose for the listeners. We want to help the audience learn first how to listen actively and restate what they heard, then to make connections, give compliments, and ask questions of the writer.

Table 7-1 illustrates an Author's Chair skills sequence that has worked well for us. Each segment in the sequence will take anywhere from several days to several weeks, depending on the degree of student success. Freeman (1998) recommends that the Author's Chair should function as the main response oppor-

Table 7-1. Sequence of Author's Chair Routine

Teaching Segments	Target Skills
1	• Author tells about topic selection. • Author reads with good volume and posture. • Audience listens attentively. • Teacher models summarization of writing.
2	• Audience summarizes writing. • Teacher models making connections to writing.
3	• Audience states connections to writing. • Teacher models giving compliments related to target skills.
4	• Audience gives compliments.
5	• Author sets purpose for listening. • Teacher models responses related to purpose for listening.
6	• Audience gives responses related to purpose for listening.
7	• Teacher models asking author questions to learn more.
8	• Audience asks questions to learn more.
9	• Teacher models revision based upon audience's questions.
10	• Audience summarizes, makes connections, gives compliments, and asks questions. • Author attempts revision based upon audience's questions.

tunity in kindergarten and the first semester of first grade. After that, the role of Author's Chair as a place for peer response will diminish as students become more adept at peer conferences. The Author's Chair will still be a place for students to celebrate a completed five-page book. We recommend that kindergarten teachers use the sequence for the first four segments; first- and second-grade teachers can use the entire progression. If second-grade students are familiar with the routines of Author's Chair because of their experiences in kindergarten and first grade, their teachers will probably use this sequence as a review before moving on to primarily a peer conference format.

Segment 1: Target Skills—Tell About Topic Selection, Summarize the Author's Piece

To illustrate how we initiate Author's Chair, we'll give scenarios from Debbie's experiences in a first-grade classroom. Although she doesn't have an Author's Chair session every day, when it is conducted, Debbie schedules time for one or two writers to contribute. Students don't have to have completed a five-page book in order to participate; they can read whatever part they choose. Debbie sets up a record-keeping system (discussed later in this chapter) to ensure that all students have an opportunity to share in the Author's Chair.

For the first 2 days, Debbie focuses primarily on the writer sitting in the Author's Chair, but she gives her first directions to the audience. "I want you to give your attention to Jose today so you can understand and enjoy his writing." Then she asks the author about his writing process. She says, "When we come to the Author's Chair, we'll give our audience some information about our writing. What's your writing about?" After Jose responds, Debbie asks, "Where did you get that idea?" Although Debbie modeled how to talk about topic selections when she wrote her own five-page book for the class, she prompts Jose to answer this question, if necessary. Then she wants the audience to be able to hear and understand each author, so she quickly models appropriate voice level and posture using a short piece she has written. As Jose reads, Debbie may need to remind him to read in a louder voice, so that everyone can hear, and to hold his book chest-high, so the audience can see his face. She also encourages him to hold up his illustrations so that all the students can see the pictures, just as she does when she reads a picture book to the class.

When Jose finishes reading his five-page book, Debbie tells the class that she will say what she remembers about the author's piece, because in a few days they will be telling what they've heard and remembered.

> Today I'm going to show you how a listener can tell what she's heard about the book after the author is finished reading in the Author's Chair. This is called <u>summarizing</u>. I heard Jose read about his Dalmatian puppy named Freckles. He wrote that he helps to take care of Freckles, and he loves him very much. Jose, is that what you wanted us to know?

After Jose confirms that Debbie has summarized his writing, Debbie shows the chart she has begun (Figure 7-1). She says:

> I've just summarized Jose's writing. I've listened to his whole piece and then told in a sentence or two what the whole piece was about. This chart will help us to remember what we do when we're at the Author's Chair. Today we learned that the listeners can summarize. I've drawn a triangle here to help us remember what summarizing is. The top of the triangle stands for the author's piece. It's long and tells a lot of details. The point of the triangle stands for the summary. The summary tells the main point of the author's piece.

Debbie also introduces the kinesthetic movement that signifies summarizing. She holds her hands spread widely above her head and says, "This is the top part of our triangle. It stands for the author's piece. We listened to the whole thing." Then she brings her hands down into a V-shape and continues, "And now we make the point of the triangle that shows the summary. We say what the piece was about in just a sentence or two. That's how we summarize."

Finally, Debbie shows the students one of the ways to celebrate the author's success. Sometimes they'll all wave their hands over their heads in celebration. Other times, they'll give a "round" of applause, clap using only index fingers, give a thumbs up, and so on.

Figure 7-1. Sharing Chart

Segment 2: Target Skill—Make Connections

Debbie has already established the routine in which the author tells where he or she got the idea for the piece; this practice will continue in all Author's Chair sessions. After she has given ample demonstrations on how to summarize a student's five-page book, Debbie expects the students to attempt the task on their own. After a student reads a piece in the Author's Chair, the author is allowed to call on three volunteers who want to summarize the piece. Debbie provides support when needed. As an alternative to having three students contribute their summarizations, Debbie often has all the students turn to their neighbor and summarize one of the pieces. This strategy allows all the students in the audience to have an opportunity to respond and practice.

Now Debbie is ready to model a new skill—making connections to one's own life, to other books, or to the world. She calls Maria to the Author's Chair. Debbie begins by stating, "Today I'm going to listen to hear if Maria's book reminds me of anything." The class then listens to Maria read her book about her mother. Debbie quickly summarizes the book and then models making connections:

> Today I'm going to make connections. I'll tell you what Maria's book reminds me of. Maria's book was about her love for her mother. She likes how her mom helps her and has fun with her. That reminds me of my mom. She has always helped me—she helped me with my schoolwork and took care of me when I was a child. Now that we're both grown-ups, we still have fun together, especially when we go shopping. When we think of how a book reminds us of something, we are making connections. You'll be doing that soon, as you listen to your friends read in the Author's Chair. I'll add "make connections" to our sharing chart. I'll draw this little two-way arrow to show that you make connections between the writing and you.

Debbie also introduces the kinesthetic movement that symbolizes the target skill. She points both index fingers inward and horizontal, and then she touches the two fingers together to show a connection.

Segment 3: Target Skill—Compliment the Author

After students begin to understand making connections to the author's writing, Debbie asks her students to respond to the writer in the Author's Chair by making connections. Again, each writer calls on three people to make connections. After the practice in making connections, students move on to complimenting the author's success in applying target skills. During these lessons, Debbie models the skill of complimenting. She first explains the skill to the students:

> It's important for authors to hear what they've done well. That's called a <u>compliment</u>. We'll compliment authors if they've done a good job of using a target skill. When we compliment an author and he knows he's done well, he will want to keep using that target skill, and his writing will become better.

Debbie's intent is to model *specific* compliments. In other words, "I like your book" is unacceptable; "I like your book because you used color words to describe" is much more specific. The class then listens to Shakeel read his five-page book. Debbie responds:

> Shakeel wrote about his family's trip to Galveston. They had fun at the beach and made a castle out of sand. I thought Shakeel did a good job of using a color word and a material word to describe the castle. He said, "I picked up my plastic shovel and scooped up some white sand." The words <u>plastic</u> and <u>white</u> give the reader more information. Good job, Shakeel! You used a color word and a material word to make your writing better. I'll add "give compliments" to our sharing chart. I'll put a little "thumbs up" to show that we like what the author did.

The kinesthetic symbol for complimenting is a "thumbs up" motion.

Segment 4: Practice in Complimenting

The next step in setting up an Author's Chair routine is to allow students to practice giving compliments. At each Author's Chair session, Debbie first reviews the class's list of target skills. Then she reminds the students to listen and hear if the author is using one of the target skills. When the author is finished reading, he calls on three classmates to give compliments. Debbie supports as needed. Again, she may have students turn to a neighbor and tell a target skill that was used by one of the writers in the Author's Chair, so that all students can participate.

Segment 5: Target Skill—Set a Purpose for Listening

First- and second-grade teachers will continue with the teaching sequence for the Author's Chair. Prior to the Author's Chair, Debbie helps one or two young authors think about a section of their writing for which they'd like to receive some help from the teacher or from their classmates. They might want to work on their lead, for example, or get feedback about the strong verbs they've used. This becomes the audience's purpose for listening

On the day she introduces the skill of setting a purpose for listening, Debbie first has a conversation with Martha about her writing. Martha is working on a piece about her birthday, and she's having trouble writing a description of her birthday cake. Debbie asks Martha to share this with the class when she's in the Author's Chair. When the students have gathered around the Author's Chair, Debbie's lesson is as follows:

> Debbie: Today we're going to learn a new way to share in the Author's Chair. It's called "setting a purpose for listening." Martha is going to read her piece about her birthday, but she's having a little bit of trouble and would like us to help. Martha, what part are you having trouble with?
>
> Martha: I'm having trouble describing my birthday cake.

> Debbie: Now I know my purpose for listening. As Martha reads her piece, I'm going to listen to her description and think of ways I might help her with her problem.

Martha reads her piece, then Debbie models giving feedback:

> Debbie: Martha said that her cake was chocolate, but she wants to include more in her description. My purpose for listening was to think of ways that I could help her. Martha, I'd like to know more about what your birthday cake looked like. Was it a tall cake or a flat cake?

Martha responds to the question. Debbie writes *tall* on a stick-on note. Martha continues to respond to the questions Debbie asks, and Debbie continues to record Martha's answers:

> Debbie: Was it round, square, or rectangular? You said it was a chocolate cake. Did it also have chocolate icing? Did it have any decorations on it? Where was it sitting?

When Debbie finishes asking questions, she gives the stick-on note to Martha and says:

> I've helped Martha to think about other words she could use to describe her birthday cake. She could say it was a tall and round cake with white fluffy icing. She could say that it was decorated with yellow and green roses and that it said, "Happy Birthday, Martha!" on it. Because Martha had set the purpose for us to listen, I was able to help her with the part on which she was stuck. Over the next few days, we'll ask the author to set a purpose for listening, and I'll show you how I can give comments to help each writer. Now I'll add "set a purpose for listening" to the sharing chart. I'll draw the face of an author while he's setting a purpose. I'll also add "help the author," and I'll draw a little light bulb. The light bulb means that we had a good idea to help the author.

Then Debbie introduces the kinesthetic movement corresponding to the target skill of helping the author. She says, "We'll tap our index finger on our head to show that we are using our brain to help the author."

As we've stressed before, Debbie is not expecting Martha to go back and use the stick-on note to revise. Although she'll model revision later in this lesson sequence, Debbie keeps in mind that her central task is to improve the writer, not the writing. Debbie has given Martha a strategy for improving her writing—adding detailed description. When Martha is composing her next piece, she can use what she's learned from the Author's Chair session about her birthday cake. Thus, she'll improve as a writer through this conversation. In fact, others will improve as well, simply by listening to the talk between Debbie and Martha.

For the next several days, Debbie has a one-on-one discussion with the students who will share in the Author's Chair. She helps them each to establish a purpose for listening. Once students become familiar with this task, the conference preceding the Author's Chair is no longer necessary.

Segment 6: Target Skill—Practice Helping the Author

After Debbie has spent several days giving feedback to the writers in the Author's Chair, she begins to release the task to the students. Each participant in the Author's Chair sets a listening purpose, and then the class is prompted to give feedback. Debbie leads the discussions until the task becomes more routine. As students give responses, Debbie writes them on a stick-on note and gives the note to the author.

Segment 7: Target Skill—Ask the Author Questions

In this lesson, Debbie models how to ask questions of the author. She begins:

> When we learned to help the author, we sometimes asked questions. Today I'm going to listen carefully to Kendrick as he reads his piece, and I'm going to think of questions I have about his writing. When he's finished, I'll ask him some questions that I wonder about or that I'm confused about, and he will answer those questions for me. I'll write the questions on a stick-on note because Kendrick might want to revisit his writing and answer some of my questions.

Kendrick shares his piece with the class, and then Debbie asks two or three questions that she thought of as she listened. She tries to model authentic questions that would be useful to Kendrick as he revises. Good questions to clear up confusions include:

> "I was confused by ___. Would you explain that to me?"
>
> "I didn't understand ___. What did you mean?"
>
> "What did you mean when you said ___?"

Debbie might ask questions to prompt elaboration, such as "What did ___ look like?" "What did you do when ___?" Once she's asked several questions, Debbie gives the stick-on note to Kendrick. She continues, "I'll add 'ask questions' to our sharing chart and draw a little question mark to help us remember that we can ask the author questions." She also teaches the kinesthetic motion of shrugging the shoulders to be a symbol of this target skill.

Segment 8: Practice in Questioning the Author

Just as Debbie did in the sixth segment, she begins to release the task to the students. Debbie leads the discussions until the questioning task becomes more routine. As students ask questions, Debbie writes them on a stick-on note and gives the note to the author.

Segment 9: Teacher Modeling of Revision

With the five-page book format, revisiting a piece is part of the daily writing process. Thus, revision is built into the act of composing. Debbie doesn't insist that students use the stick-on notes from an Author's Chair session to revise their current pieces because, as we've said before, she wants to improve the writer, not just one particular piece of writing. Debbie understands that discussions that stem from Author's Chair sessions give students a way to talk about their writing that will help them to improve each subsequent piece.

Debbie wants, however, to give students some experience with revision based on feedback from the audience. To begin this mini-lesson, Debbie refers to her current piece of writing. After she has read it to the class, she asks, "Are there any questions or confusions you have about my piece?" As students respond, she writes their responses on a stick-on note. When students have finished responding, Debbie continues, "You have given me some good ideas to improve this piece. Authors will often get ideas from friends and then revisit their piece using their friends' ideas. That's what I'm going to do now." She uses one or more of the revision techniques that the class has already studied to revise her piece based on the feedback from the students. (Revision techniques include adding information with a caret [chapter 2], rearranging pages [chapter 3], and using spider legs [chapter 3].)

Segment 10: Revision Based on Feedback

Debbie begins this lesson by reviewing the sharing chart in Figure 7-1:

> We've learned lots of ways to help our authors when they share in the Author's Chair. This chart will help us to remember them. We can summarize by telling what the piece was about. We can make connections or we can give the author compliments. Sometimes authors will want our help, so they'll set the purpose for listening. Then we can make comments that might help them to improve their piece. Finally, we can ask questions related to things we're confused about or things we want to know more about. This might help the writer revisit his piece and improve it. Today when Robbie reads to us, he'll first set a purpose for listening. Then when we respond, we can do any of the things on this chart. We can summarize, make connections, give compliments, give help, or ask questions.

As the Author's Chair routine continues, Debbie prompts and supports as the tasks become established.

Sustaining the Author's Chair Routine

Once Debbie has completed the above set of Author's Chair lessons, she works to sustain the routine throughout the year. As we've stated before, the Author's Chair routine will be the main response opportunity for kindergartners and first graders in the first semester. After that, the role of Author's Chair will diminish as you help students to become more proficient with peer conferences. However, even when peer conferences become the main response option for students, Author's Chair can still be used when you want the whole class to celebrate a particular piece of writing or discuss a specific writing technique. There's no need for every child to attend each Author's Chair session, however, nor is it necessary for the Author's Chair to be conducted at the end of writing workshop. Freeman (1998) suggests that while students are writing, you say, "___ needs an audience." At that point, students choose whether they wish to become part of the Author's Chair audience.

Benefits of the Author's Chair

Although it's uncommon for young writers to revise after receiving feedback from their peers, we're sure that you will see the benefits of the Author's Chair routine once you've used it in your classroom. As a result of your effective Author's Chair, you will see the following (Freeman, 1998):

- ✓ Young writers understand that others see that their words have value.

- ✓ Each author has the opportunity to hear his or her own work.

- ✓ Students have the chance to catch errors when they read their piece aloud.

- ✓ Students know each other's topics and get ideas for topics of their own.

- ✓ Students practice listening attentively.

- ✓ Vocabulary expands.

- ✓ Writing behaviors repeat when writers are complimented.

- ✓ When students are complimented for using a target skill, others are motivated to apply target skills in their own writing.

- ✓ A sense of community is enhanced.

- ✓ The teacher gets another chance to give writing advice.

✓ There is an integration of the four language arts: speaking, listening, reading, and writing.

✓ You are rewarded when you hear that students have applied the skills you've taught.

✓ You have laid the foundation so that students can transition into peer conferences.

Informal Response Opportunities

In addition to the formal Author's Chair, which you control, students will have other opportunities to share their work in more informal settings. Throughout the sustained writing portion of writing workshop, students will spontaneously read parts of their writing to their classmates. We also require that writers who are finished with their books first share with a classmate before coming to us for a final conference. Our most frequent use of informal response opportunities occurs at the end of the sustained writing time. On the days when we don't plan to have an Author's Chair session, we often pair students so that they have a chance to read part of their writing to a classmate. We use several different pairing options so that students will share with many of their peers. We might ask the students to read to the person sitting next to them. Sometimes we select Popsicle sticks, each with a student's name written on it, to determine the partners. A favorite activity is "Mix, Freeze." We teach our students to walk quietly around the room with their writing until they hear us say, "Freeze." Then they "Stop, drop, and share" with the person nearest to them. These sharing options are designed so that students simply read a part of their writing to their partners; no response is required. We'll discuss peer responses in the next section.

Conferences

Peer Conferences

Peer conferences are just a short step from the informal sharing described above, but in peer conferences students are giving feedback to each other. You've already laid the groundwork for peer conferences if you've taught about target skills and Author's Chair (Figure 7-2). Peer conferences will not generally result in revision; young writers don't often change their pieces in response to feedback. The value of peer conferences is that they do the following:

✓ Help to build community as young learners work together

✓ Reinforce the language and habit of authors

✓ Teach independence so students don't become reliant
on the teacher

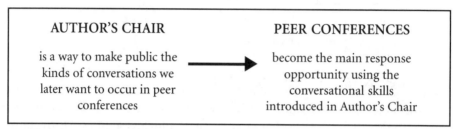

Figure 7-2. Moving to Peer Conferences

Just as with any new skill, you must explicitly teach the procedures you want
your students to follow as they participate in peer conferences. We introduce
peer conferences after students have become familiar with Author's Chair routines. By this time, students understand that listeners can summarize, make
connections, give compliments, help the author, and ask questions. Students
have also practiced recognizing when an author has used a target skill, and they
understand the use of did-it dots.

We demonstrate our first few peer conferences using the fishbowl technique
as a mini-lesson. With this technique, two students sit in the middle surrounded
by a circle of their classmates. The students in the middle will have their peer
conference in the "fishbowl," and the other children are observers of the conference. The teacher sits nearby so she can prompt the peer partners to apply the
skills they've learned in the Author's Chair. She has a small box of did-it dots
close at hand.

We'll use Shirl's first-grade class as an example. Jarvis and Stephanie have
both agreed to participate in the fishbowl. Shirl has selected these peer partners
because she knows that they will not be inhibited as they confer in front of their
classmates. The rest of the students gather around them in a circle. Jarvis will be
the author and Stephanie will provide feedback. Shirl begins:

> Today we're making a fishbowl. Have you ever seen a goldfish
> inside a fishbowl? You were on the outside looking in. That's
> like our fishbowl is today. Jarvis and Stephanie are inside the
> fishbowl and the rest of you are on the outside looking in.
> Jarvis and Stephanie are going to help us learn how to do a
> peer conference. Do any of you know what a peer conference
> is?

Students make predictions, and then Shirl continues:

> A peer conference is like a miniature Author's Chair. Instead of
> the whole class working together, it will be just Stephanie and

> Jarvis. One of them is the author and the other is the audi-
> ence. Today Jarvis will read his piece to Stephanie, and
> Stephanie will talk with him about it. That's just what we do
> when we are having an Author's Chair session.

Shirl reminds her students about the sharing chart that they've already used (see Fig. 7-1). "Whenever we've had our Author's Chair, the author first sets a purpose for listening. Jarvis, do you have anything you'd like Stephanie to listen for?" Jarvis sets a purpose for Stephanie. Shirl continues, "Stephanie, you'll use this chart to help you. First you'll summarize what Jarvis's piece is about. Then you can make a connection, give a compliment, give him some help, or ask him some questions." Jarvis reads his piece, and then Stephanie provides feedback. Shirl prompts and supports Stephanie. When Jarvis and Stephanie have concluded their discussion, Shirl says:

> When you're done with a peer conference, the listener can
> pick one dot out of this box. Then you can put a did-it dot on
> the author's writing. Stephanie, think about a target skill that
> Jarvis did really, really well. What was it?

After Stephanie has answered the question, she gets a did-it dot, labels it, and places it in the appropriate spot in Jarvis's book. Shirl thanks Jarvis and Stephanie and tells the class that they'll be doing the fishbowl technique for a few more days to help everyone know what to do during a peer conference.

Each day, Shirl tries to lessen her degree of support as students assume more of the task on their own. Once Shirl senses that students understand the purpose and routine for peer conferences, she releases the task to the students. She "eavesdrops" on the conversation of partners as they confer and steps in when she sees them struggling. In addition, she holds fishbowl conferences occasionally to review and reinforce the procedures.

There's no one best way to select peer partners. We teach our students to ask their classmates, "Will you be my conference partner?" The student can nod for "yes," shake her head for "no," or hold up one finger, meaning "Yes, I'll help, but give me 1 minute to finish up my thought." The peer partners then move to a quiet place in the classroom and sit knee to knee on the floor or side by side in chairs. We copy the chart in Figure 7-1 and place it in each student's writing folder as a support for the partners as they confer. You'll want to ensure that the partnerships result in successful conferences. You may need to step in if the partners are off task or unproductive.

Peer conferences are limited in the support they give young writers. Although such conversations are beneficial, primary students aren't trained writing teachers. The conferences can reinforce the skills you've taught, but they can't provide the specific feedback required to move a writer into new understandings. Thus teacher-led conferences are essential for increasing each student's knowledge of a variety of writing techniques.

Teacher-Led Conferences

Entire books have been written on conducting writing conferences. This is not a simple topic, and it is not an easy job to do well. We will summarize here how we manage writing conferences with our primary students, and we will share information from some of the professional books that we've found helpful. For a more in-depth discussion of teacher-led writing conferences, see *How's It Going?: A Practical Guide to Conferring With Student Writers* by Carl Anderson (2000).

We haven't yet met a teacher who feels that he or she is an expert on conferring with student writers. Every time our confidence level rises, there comes a challenge for which we're not prepared. Anderson equates writing conferences with conversations. When we think of conferences in that way, they don't seem so daunting. Anderson (p. 7) lists several characteristics in which conferring is similar to conversing:

- ✓ Conferences have a point to them.
- ✓ Conferences have a predictable structure.
- ✓ In conferences, we pursue a line of thinking with students.
- ✓ Teachers and students have conversational roles in conferences.
- ✓ In conferences, we show students that we care about them.

During our writing conferences, our goal is to listen carefully and respond honestly. That's not any different from the conversations we have with our family and friends. The major difference is that in writing conferences we give feedback that will help the writer to improve.

Lucy Calkins (1994) gives one piece of advice that has had a significant impact on our thoughts about conferring. She says:

> If we can keep only one thing in mind—and I fail at this half the time—it is that we are teaching the writer and not the writing. Our decisions must be guided by "what might help this writer" rather than "what might help this writing" (p. 228).

This quote helped us to realize that writing conferences are challenging to do, and it's okay not to do them perfectly. Most important, Calkins helped us to realize that it's not our job to work with the writer in order to "fix" his writing. It's our job to talk with the writer about one or two things that he will internalize and be able to use in his next piece. This has helped us to look at our students' writing differently. Instead of seeing all the things we could help the writer with (and there are many things that primary writers need), we consider all we know about the student and pick a powerful issue that will help the writer the next time she writes. A focus on content *always* takes precedence over a focus on mechanics.

Fletcher and Portalupi (1998) offer some practical tips for conducting writing conferences. They suggest that we do the following:

- ✓ Respond first as a reader, not as a teacher.
- ✓ Have a positive, inviting demeanor while maintaining high standards.
- ✓ Make an effort to understand what the writer is trying to do.
- ✓ Lower your ambitions by teaching one or two things in each piece.

We like these suggestions. They remind us that we are part of the writing community. We do have an obligation to teach, but our obligation to honor our students as writers is equally important.

Roving Conferences

Most of our conference opportunities occur as students are doing their sustained writing. We interact with students as they write, no matter where they are in the writing process. Avery (1993) calls these *roving conferences* because we walk around the room and stop routinely to discuss a student's writing. In addition, we need to have a conference when a student has finished a piece, and we give feedback before that student begins a different five-page-book. Either of these two conference formats can be practiced using the fishbowl technique described in the section on peer conferences.

As students are writing, we walk through the classroom, stopping to hold brief conferences (usually 5 minutes or less) with individuals. In the past, we've had students come to us at a special "conference" table. We now either kneel by the student's desk or pull up a small chair. It's important that we are at the student's eye level. By conducting our conference at the student's desk, we've found that other students around us sometimes listen and learn from the conversation that is occurring.

Anderson (2000) shares the two roles that transpire during a writing conference. First, the student is in the lead role as she sets an agenda by describing her writing work. After that, the teacher is in the lead as he discusses his responses to the student's writing. Using one of two introductory statements (Figure 7-3), our first task is to listen to what the child has to say. You may want to write these two questions on an index card and carry them around with you until you feel more secure initiating writing conferences. Once the student responds to the introductory statement, she reads her writing to us. We summarize, make connections, and ask questions that will clarify and deepen our understanding. Then we assume the lead role as we give compliments or prompts related to target skills. Our basic rule is to first address the writer's content and then perhaps address a written convention. Often we will only listen to a child's reading of his piece, and not look at it at first, so that we can focus deeply on the content and the mechanical errors don't distract us from the message.

Introductory Statements

Tell me about your writing. (Avery, 1993)

or

What are you doing today as a writer? (Anderson, 2000)

Figure 7-3. Introductory Statements for Roving Conferences

Ray (1999) discusses the interrelationship of assessment, curriculum, and instruction, and the importance of this interrelationship as we conduct good writing conferences. When we first sit down with a writer and ask her to set a purpose for listening and then read her piece, our goal is to determine what she is trying to do with her writing. That's *assessment*—we're assessing what the child is attempting. The next step is curricular—we consider what we know about appropriate target skills that we could use to help this particular writer at this particular time. This step draws upon our knowledge of *curriculum*—the skills, strategies, and writing techniques that are suitable for young writers. As Ray asserts, "The more you know of curriculum, the more opportunities you find to teach in very contextual ways in a writing workshop" (p. 248). Finally, the last step of a good writing conference is *instruction*. Once we've determined the skill, strategy, or writing technique we want to discuss with our young author, we teach it. The art of conducting a writing conference is to keep these three components, and their sequence, in mind as we have a conversation with each writer.

When we first began holding writing conferences, we were careful not to hurt a writer's feelings by being too assertive. We thought that being firm about what we wanted our writers to try would discourage their creativity. Over time, we have decided to take a more active role. Ray discusses how her experiences with an editor as she co-authored a professional book helped her to better understand the teacher's role during writing conferences. She states:

> The experience was, to put it mildly, revolutionary for me as a teacher of writing. I can define what our editor did for us quite simply: She looked at our drafts to see what we were trying to do, and then she made suggestions along the way for how to do it even *better* It was obvious from the start that she knew a lot about writing, and this gave us the confidence to entrust our writing to her. (p. 249)

Now we feel more comfortable encouraging our students to improve their pieces by offering suggestions, helping them to craft their piece, and sometimes simply insisting that they try a new technique. Our assistance, however, is always within the context of what we've previously taught. It is unreasonable to expect children to try writing techniques that are unfamiliar to them.

The roving conference provides a good occasion for teachers to celebrate their students' accomplishments in writing. When we hear a nice turn of phrase or observe a student trying a new technique, for example, we not only compliment the writer privately, we celebrate publicly. We highlight their work in front of the class, usually during the end-of-workshop share session. Anderson (2000) calls this "making the writer famous."

Final Conferences

Before students come to us for a conference when they've finished a piece of writing, we insist that they first meet with a partner for a peer conference. After the peer conference, we sit down to discuss the child's writing. We've already had several roving conferences with him, so our conference focuses on goal setting. We thumb through the writing again and consult our conference notes in order to refresh our memory of the content. We ask the writer, "What did you try in this piece to help make you a better writer?" After we discuss this question, we ask him to set a goal for his next book. We talk about what he'd like to try next and what we'd like him to use, too. Next, we write both goals (his and ours) on the back of his new five-page book. To write the goals, Debbie prepares labels on her home computer similar to the illustration in Figure 7-4.

Finally, we remind the student to select a new topic, ensure that he has enough information for five pages, and begin a new five-page book.

Figure 7-4.   Goals Sticker

Record Keeping

We confess that neither of us was very good with record keeping. We always thought that we would remember which students we had conferred with, what their topics were, and what the response was. We were sure we would remember who had shared in the Author's Chair. We learned from our mistake, however, and now keep a clipboard with us so that we can jot brief notes about each writing workshop session. We make one sheet per student. The recording of notes helps us to summarize the interactions with each child so that we can refer to them for future conferences and for assessment and grading purposes. We also record the type of interaction—a roving conference, a final conference, or an Author's Chair sharing. An example of Debbie's record keeping is shown in Figure 7-5. After we've filled up a page, we transfer it to the individual writing folders that we keep on each child. These folders contain conference notes and any additional documents that contribute to our understanding of our students as writers.

Name	Shakeel		
Date	**Type**		**Notes**
10/11	RC	complimented use of ∧ to add details	
10/16	RC	is experimenting w/ speech bubbles – discussed how to write it as dialogue	
10/17	AC	shared 1st 3 pgs – worked on volume	
10/22	RC	stuck on ending – discussed possible options	
10/25	FC	said he'd learned about quotation marks – set goals: 1) add more details (his) 2) revisit • put in periods (mine)	

RC = Roving conference
AC = Author's chair
FC = Final conference

Figure 7-5. Record Keeping

There are many different formats that are available for record keeping. We've outlined what has worked well for us. (A blank record keeping form is found in the appendixes.)We recommend that you find a format that works best for you.

Chapter

Assessment and Small-Group Instruction

We believe that both the processes and the products of composing are important. Both guide us to see strengths and needs as our students move through the stages of writing development. Therefore, we assess the processes our students use as they write as well as the products they create.

—Susan Mandel Glazer and Carol Smullen Brown, *Portfolios and Beyond*

When Debbie was about 7 years old, she took swimming lessons with her Brownie troop. Some of the girls in the troop were natural athletes and already seemed to swim like dolphins, some had spent lots of time around a pool and could swim competently, and others were fairly inexperienced swimmers. Debbie was the worst student in the group. Not only did she share her mother's fear of water, she had also missed several days of the 2-week course. The instructors realized that the "one size fits all" lessons they had planned weren't appropriate for this group and that they would need to adapt their instruction to accommodate the different skill levels.

Writing instruction is similar. As you examine your students' writing, you will undoubtedly observe that each student's writing differs from that of his or her peers. Some students will soak up all of your lessons and confidently excel. Other students will experiment tentatively as they become better writers. Still others will lag behind their peers and worry you because of their lack of progress.

In addition to whole-group mini-lessons and individual writing conferences, small-group instruction focusing on specific needs will benefit all of your students. Small groups stem from careful assessment of student needs.

Assessment to Guide Instruction

Two purposes of assessment are paramount (Rickards & Cheek, 1999). First, we assess student writing so that we can report progress to the parents, the school administration, and the public. Second, and in our opinion the most important, we assess student progress to guide our instruction. In chapter 7 we discussed the "on the spot" assessment you'll do as the first step in any teacher-led writing conference. This chapter will deal with the more formal assessments you'll do periodically to evaluate each student's progress. We'll touch briefly on the first purpose, but we'll primarily address the second: informing instruction. Two ways to formally assess writing are useful: considering developmental stages and utilizing rubrics.

Developmental Stages

One way to examine your students' written work is to consider the developmental stages of primary writers. By looking at writing in this way, you can observe the concepts and principles that each student understands about written text and uses in his or her writing. With this information, you can provide more accurate information to parents and plan small-group instruction based on developmental writing needs.

Categories of Writing Development

We have identified four broad categories in writing development: (a) oral message writers, (b) beginning writers, (c) developing writers, and (d) experienced writers. Within these categories are narrower stages that more distinctly describe writers and their developmental levels.

Oral message writers. Children whose writing falls in the first category don't yet understand that writing involves words that a reader must interpret. These children either draw, scribble, write letterlike forms, or write random letters. The reader needs the child to tell the message orally. Children who are oral message writers are usually 3 to 5 years old.

Beginning writers. Children who are in the second category of writing development are beginning to understand that writing must contain letters and words. These children may copy environmental print or use only initial consonants to write their message. Further along in this category are children who are experimenting with final consonants and are using, but confusing, vowel sounds. Children who are beginning writers are generally in kindergarten or first grade.

Developing writers. This category includes children who are beginning to understand writing conventions and use some basic writing strategies. Their knowledge of writing mechanics and spelling is increasing. Their text length is also increasing, and the writing is becoming organized. The writers in this category may attempt to revise, usually by addition or substitution. These students may be experimenting with different genres and forms of writing. Children who are developing writers are generally first- through third-grade students.

Experienced writers. Students generally begin this category of writing around fourth grade, although people with limited writing experience may never reach this category. These writers have mastered most of the conventions of writing and can write a well-organized and elaborate piece. These writers use voice, have a sense of their audience, and can easily revise to improve their writing.

Table 8-1 summarizes these four broad categories of writing development.

Table 8-1. Categories of Writing Development

Category	Description
Oral Message Writer	The writer puts marks on the page and calls it writing, but a reader cannot interpret the writing. The writer expresses the message orally.
Beginning Writer	The writer is beginning to understand that writing contains letters and words. The reader may need help to interpret the writing.
Developing Writer	The writer understands many of the conventions of writing. The message is easy for a reader to interpret. The writing lacks complexity.
Experienced Writer	The writer uses complex sentences and the writing is well developed. The writer unconsciously applies most conventions and experiments with different forms, genres, and word choice.

Stages Within Categories

Within the broad categories are several narrower groups of writing stages. The oral message category has students at four stages: drawing, scribbling, letterlike forms, and random letters. Stages of the beginning writer category are word copier, initial consonants, and phonetic speller. The developing writer goes through stages of understanding conventions and attempting revision. Writers who are experienced are either in the skilled stage or the fully fluent stage. Figure 8-1 illustrates the continuum of stages that writers move through on their way to becoming experienced writers.

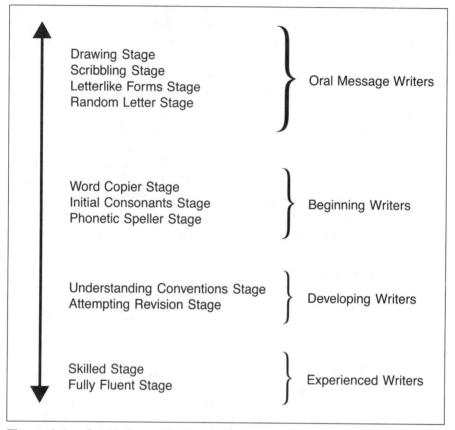

Drawing Stage
Scribbling Stage
Letterlike Forms Stage
Random Letter Stage
} Oral Message Writers

Word Copier Stage
Initial Consonants Stage
Phonetic Speller Stage
} Beginning Writers

Understanding Conventions Stage
Attempting Revision Stage
} Developing Writers

Skilled Stage
Fully Fluent Stage
} Experienced Writers

Figure 8-1.   Continuum of Writing Development

We don't want to leave the impression that these stages are rigid indicators of writing development. Students may exhibit characteristics of several writing stages in a single piece of writing. Instead, we use these flexibly, looking to see what the writing tells us about each child's writing development and what we need to model, teach, and prompt him or her to try next.

Oral Message Stages

Drawing. Children at this stage of writing development draw instead of write. They tell their message orally, interpreting the drawing as text. They may begin to write the letters in their name. A writing sample at the drawing stage from Kelsey (3 years old) is shown in Figure 8-2. She described the picture as "Grandpa."

Scribbling. On first glance, it seems as if the writer in Figure 8-2 is more advanced than the writer in Figure 8-3, which shows an example of the scribbling stage. It seems logical that a child would make random scribbles before making an obvious illustration. The rationale for placing the scribbling stage after the drawing stage is apparent when we consider the child's purpose. If the child simply scribbled on a page, then it's considered just scribbling, not a stage of writing. However, if he has already passed from the drawing stage and is beginning to realize that writing is not just drawing, he is more advanced than the child in the drawing stage. These are the children who say, "Watch me write," and then scribble on the paper. Scribbling stage writers may be experimenting with writing their names.

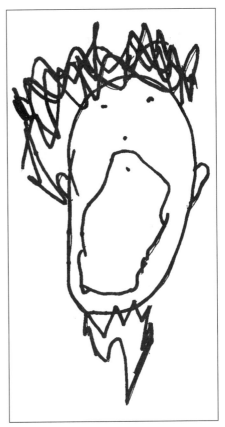

Figure 8-2. Drawing Stage

Letterlike forms. Children in this stage are noticing that writing isn't scribbling but has standard shapes that are repeated within the writing. Their writing contains shapes that are letterlike in their form. These children may know how to write their own names. An example is shown in Figure 8-4.

Random letters. These children have reached the point where they see that writing is made up of individual letters. However, they have no usable knowledge of letter-sound relationships, so the letters they write are random. They can usually write their own names, and their other writing may have a preponderance of letters

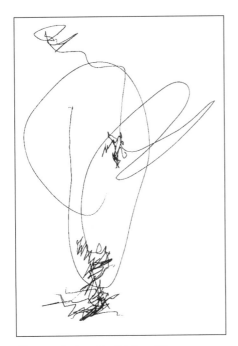

Figure 8-3. Scribbling Stage

that are found in their names. Maria's writing in Figure 8-5 is a good example of a kindergartner's writing at the random letters stage.

Figure 8-4. Letterlike Forms Stage

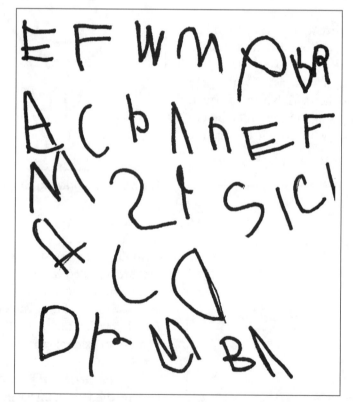

Figure 8-5. Random Letters Stage

The characteristics of writers in the oral message stage are listed in Table 8-2.

Table 8-2. Stages of Oral Message Writers

Category	Stage	Characteristics of Writers
Oral Message	Drawing	• Draws as writing • May attempt to write own name • Expresses message orally
	Scribbling	• Scribbles as writing • May attempt to write name • Expresses message orally
	Letterlike Forms	• Writes shapes that are similar to letters • May be able to write own name • Expresses message orally
	Random Letters	• Understands that people write using letters • Writes random letters or letters found in name • May be able to write own name • Expresses message orally

Beginning Writer Stages

Word copier. Children in this stage of writing development now understand that people write using words. They regularly copy environmental print but can't usually identify the meaning of the words they copy. They use mostly uppercase letters and can probably write their own names. Figure 8-6 shows the writing of a kindergartner in the word copier stage. Akeem copied the words and illustrations from an alphabet chart in his classroom.

Initial consonants. These students are developing knowledge of sound-symbol relationships, and their writing shows their use of initial consonants. They don't yet distinguish between the

Figure 8-6. Word Copier Stage

proper use of upper- and lowercase letters, so their writing contains a mixture of forms. These children now understand the relationship between their writing and their message, but they usually write only one sentence. They are aware that writing proceeds from left to right and from top to bottom. Figure 8-7 shows Maggie's writing at the initial consonants stage. It says: *I love, love, love mom.*

Figure 8-7.   Initial Consonants Stage

Phonetic speller. Students who are phonetic spellers use the correct consonant for beginning and final sounds most of the time. They use, but confuse, medial vowel sounds—vowels merely serve as a placeholder to represent a sound of which they're unsure. They rarely use long vowel spelling patterns. Their knowledge of conventional spelling is increasing, and they're often using capital letters and ending punctuation correctly. These children are beginning to develop a sense of story, and their writing has multiple sentences. In Figure 8-8, Richard, a

Figure 8-8.   Phonetic Speller Stage

first grader, writes: "If you hit her on the head she will bite you. Beagle will bite but my other dog will not bite and he likes to jump on the tree." Richard is in the phonetic speller stage of writing development.

The characteristics of the beginning writer stage are found in Table 8-3.

Table 8-3. Stages of Beginning Writer

Category	Stage	Characteristics of Writers
Beginning Writer	Word Copier	• Understands that people write using words • Copies environmental print, but the words often have no meaning for the writer • Uses mostly uppercase letters • Probably can write own name
	Initial Consonants	• Uses initial consonants to express message • Uses mostly uppercase letters • Successfully transfers ideas to print • Usually writes just one sentence • Writes from left to right and top to bottom • Can write own name
	Phonetic Speller	• Uses initial and ending consonants • Uses, but confuses, medial vowel sounds • Does not use long-vowel patterns • Begins to write some sight words • Successfully transfers ideas to print • Writes pieces with multiple sentences • Begins to develop a sense of story

Developing Writer Stages

Understands conventions. Writers in this stage are becoming more adept with the conventions of writing. When spelling, the writers have a bank of known words, use short vowels correctly, and use long-vowel patterns, though not always correctly. They usually use capital letters and ending punctuation correctly. These children write organized pieces with multiple sentences and a beginning, a middle, and an end. They begin to use details to develop their ideas. See Figure 8-9 for an example of the understands conventions stage. This is one page out of Sarah's five-page book about her trip to the beach. It says, "We made a beautiful sand castle. Then my dad came with us."

Attempts revision. Spelling becomes more conventional in this stage. Children are usually able to spell long-vowel patterns correctly and they have a large bank of known words. Students in this stage consider making their writing better by rereading and self-correcting and by revising through addition or substitution. Their pieces are longer, with an organizational structure that is evident. Figure 8-10 shows a writing sample in the attempts revision stage. On the first

Figure 8-9. Understands Conventions Stage

page of her five-page book about her family, Linda (a first grader) shows that she has attempted revision. It says: "My family is very nice. I gave a rabbit to my nice sister and my sister gave me something back. My other sister likes to play with me lots more but she doesn't take turns." She has added *very, lot,* and *nice.* We can see that she has attempted several spellings of *nice* before deciding upon the correct one.

Figure 8-10. Attempts Revision Stage

Table 8-4 summarizes the characteristics of the developing writer stage.

Table 8-4. Stages of Developing Writer

Category	Stage	Characteristics of Writers
Developing Writer	Understands Conventions	• Uses short vowels correctly • Uses, but confuses, long-vowel patterns • Is developing a bank of known spelling words • Usually uses capital letters and ending punctuation correctly • Writes pieces with multiple sentences and with a beginning, middle, and end • Begins to use details to develop ideas
	Attempts Revision	• Is usually able to use vowel patterns when spelling • Has a large bank of known spelling words • Will reread and self-correct • Will revise by addition • May revise by substitution • Pieces become longer with an organizational structure that is evident

Experienced Writer Stages

Skilled. Skilled writers are fully competent and exhibit mastery of most of the necessary elements to produce a good piece of writing. They revise easily, use detailed elaboration, and experiment with word choice. Their writing is clearly organized and flows well. These writers use voice and

The little Rabbit

One day a little rabbit told his mother that he wanted to move away so his mother said, "Its ob if you run away." His mom said that cause she was a blind rabbit mother. So anyway the rabbit ran away so the mom creeped up creep creep creep creep creep creep. She kept on kreeping until

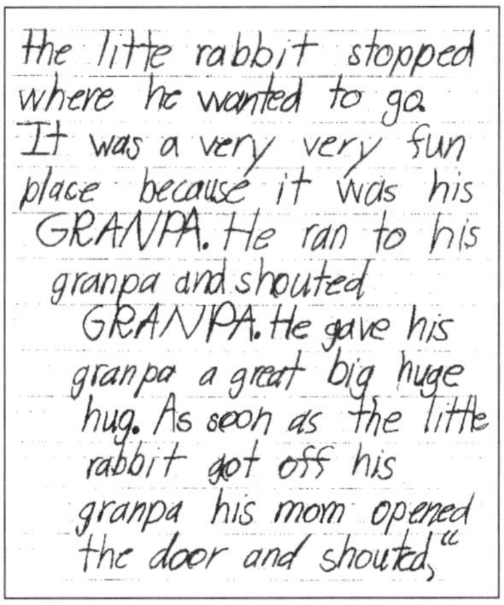

the litle rabbit stopped where he wanted to go. It was a very very fun place because it was his GRANPA. He ran to his granpa and shouted GRANPA. He gave his granpa a great big huge hug. As seon as the little rabbit got off his granpa his mom opened the door and shouted, "

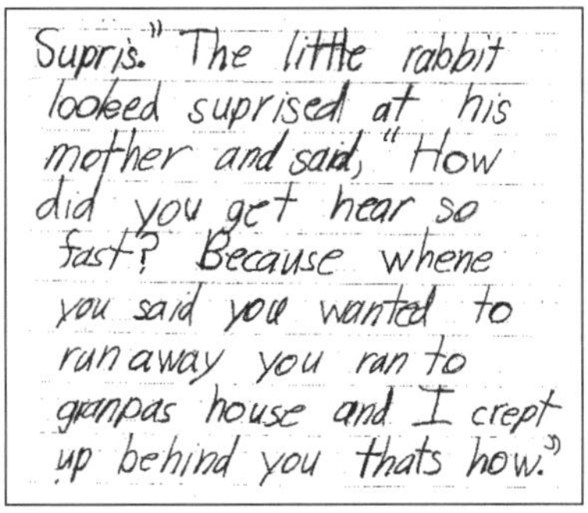

Supris." The little rabbit looked suprised at his mother and said, "How did you get hear so fast? Because whene you said you wanted to run away you ran to granpas house and I crept up behind you thats how."

Figure 8-11. Skilled Stage

demonstrate an awareness of audience. Their purpose for writing is evident. Most writers reach their writing peak at this stage of development. Figure 8-11 is a sample of Michael's writing at the skilled stage.

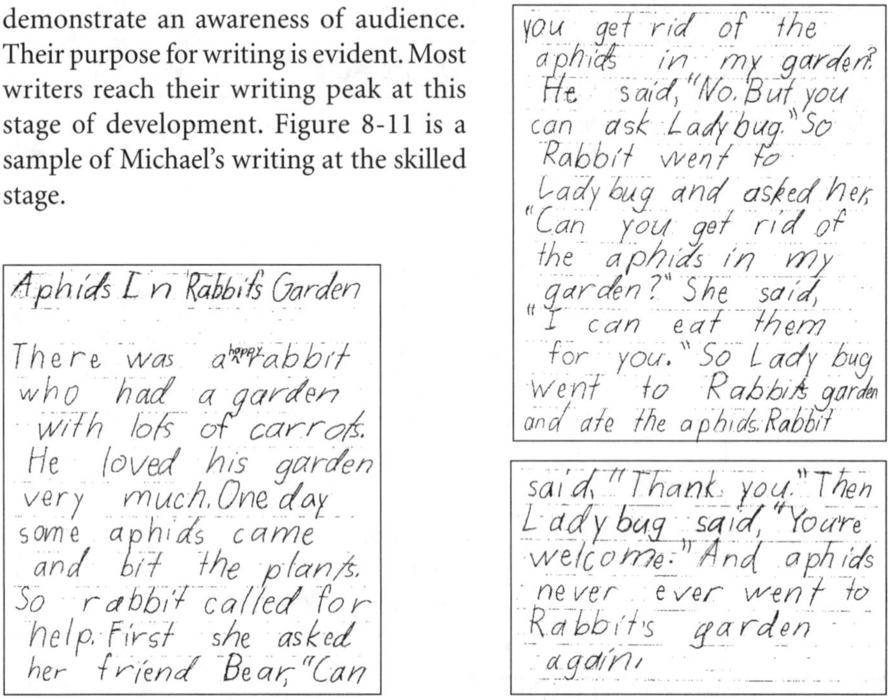

> Aphids I n Rabbits Garden
>
> There was a ʰᵃᵖᵖʸrabbit who had a garden with lots of carrots. He loved his garden very much. One day some aphids came and bit the plants. So rabbit called for help. First she asked her friend Bear, "Can

> you get rid of the aphids in my garden? He said, "No. But you can ask Lady bug." So Rabbit went to Lady bug and asked her, "Can you get rid of the aphids in my garden?" She said, "I can eat them for you." So Lady bug went to Rabbits garden and ate the aphids. Rabbit

> said, "Thank you." Then Lady bug said, "You're welcome." And aphids never ever went to Rabbit's garden again.

Figure 8-12. Fully Fluent Stage

Table 8-5. Stages of Experienced Writer

Category	Stage	Characteristics of Writers
Experienced Writer	Skilled	• Has mastered most conventions of writing • Begins to use different forms of writing • Revises easily • Details are elaborated • Experiments with word choice • Organization is clear and writing flows well • Purpose is evident • Demonstrates an awareness of audience • Uses voice
	Fully Fluent	• Has mastered conventions of writing • Uses different forms effectively • Revises easily • Organization is clear and writing flows well • Establishes and maintains a clear purpose • Demonstrates an awareness of audience • Chooses writing as a leisure activity • Clearly expresses self with passion and voice • Uses effective elaboration throughout piece

Fully fluent. A fully fluent writer is one who writes with flair. These writers choose writing as a leisure activity and clearly express themselves with passion and voice. They have mastered the conventions of writing and easily employ different forms for different purposes. Elaboration is used in an organized and effective manner. Primary writers are unlikely to reach this stage of writing development. However, Randy, a talented writer in first grade, composed the story shown in Figure 8-12.

A summary of the characteristics of the experienced writer stage is found in Table 8-5.

Rubrics

Because the assessment of writing is generally a subjective endeavor, traditional objective tests are usually inadequate for providing the information necessary to guide our writing instruction. We have found that our preferred method of writing assessment is rubrics.

Rubrics are assessment tools that use levels of proficiency to delineate the differences among student writers. Rubrics have several advantages that make them excellent tools for classroom writing assessment (Rickards & Cheek, 1999):

✓ They require the careful reflection of the teacher to identify the important skills and strategies to assess.

✓ They allow students to be informed about the teacher's expectations and criteria for assessment.

✓ They easily translate into a tool for student self-assessment.

✓ They foster collaboration as teachers work together to develop rubrics.

We use rubrics to assess each student's success at "hitting the target" related to the target skill being taught. We also use rubrics to assess students' writing processes and their written products. Using a rubric effectively assumes that the criteria to be assessed and the levels of proficiency used are established before the writing is done so that both the teacher and the students understand the goals they are working toward and can evaluate works in progress (Routman, 2000).

Regarding the process and the product, Avery (1993) states:

> The final product could be examined in isolation, but the context surrounding any piece of writing enriched my understanding of a child's development....I began looking at growth over time and considering all that children said and did as they wrote. Product *and* process were essential to documenting student growth. (p. 399–400)

That's what we mean by process and product—looking at *how* the author composes the piece as well as *what* the author ultimately writes. An overemphasis on one or the other could lead to a misleading assessment of a child's writing skill. Therefore, the assessments that we gather on each child must have a balance between process and product. We've used rubrics effectively to maintain this balance.

Consider the sample rubric in Figure 8-13. We use this rubric for our first

---

Name _____   Date _____

Topic _____

SCORING RUBRIC

TARGET SKILLS: The writer . . .   SCORE

   1. Planned five pages   _____

   2. Stayed on topic   _____

   3. Attempted to add details   _____

   4. Matched words and illustration   _____

   5. Spelled word wall words correctly   _____

   6. Used sound-spelling to spell unfamiliar words   _____

SCORING CRITERIA

   4 = apparent throughout the piece; the writer's use of this target skill was effective

   3 = apparent through most of the piece; the writer's use of this target skill was generally effective

   2 = apparent through some of the piece; the writer's use of this target skill was minimally effective

   1 = attempt to use target skill apparent through some of the piece but not used effectively

   0 = writer did not attempt to use this target skill

COMMENTS ON BACK

Figure 8-13. Sample Scoring Rubric

formal assessment after we have introduced and worked with five-page books. The development of this rubric required our careful reflection to determine the target skills we wanted to assess and our consideration of the levels of proficiency we wanted to use. It can easily be used to promote student self-assessment. (We'll discuss self-assessment later in this chapter.) With a few adaptations, it's relatively easy to share this rubric with students. In addition, we like the format of this rubric because of its ease of use and its flexibility.

When we determined the target skills included on this rubric, we thought about the most important skills we've taught and what's appropriate for students in our grade level. We included a balance between process and product. We chose a 5-point scale to distinguish among the different levels of proficiency for each target skill. This format is flexible because we change the target skills as the year progresses. We add or delete target skills as we introduce, practice, and support new skills. For example, later in the school year, we might change the target skills to the following:

✓ Considers different leads

✓ Uses strong verbs

✓ Uses ending punctuation correctly

✓ Experiments with dialogue

✓ Summarizes partner's piece during peer conferences

✓ Makes connections to author's piece during peer conferences or Author's Chair

We keep a template of this rubric on our computer so that we can easily change the target skills as needed. As you can see, the target skills that we want to assess change as our curriculum and instruction change.

About every 3 or 4 weeks, we sit down with our students' current writings, our anecdotal notes, and copies of scoring rubrics. We carefully consider each child's progress and assign a score that is our best judgment about the child's work as a writer related to the target skills on our rubric. It is subjective, but we feel confident that we've gathered enough evidence to support our conclusions. Each rubric takes about 5 minutes to complete; a class of 20 students takes about 2 hours. The time we spend on this assessment is a worthwhile investment because of its role in informing our teaching decisions and allowing for small-group instruction.

Small-Group Instruction

In our classrooms, we have a variety of grouping options. Sometimes we meet with the whole class as we conduct our mini-lessons. Other times, we meet one-on-one with students as we hold writing conferences. Still other times, we use flexible groupings to meet with a few students at a time, based upon their current needs. Developmental stages and rubrics provide the tools to help us make teaching decisions to meet the needs of each young writer in our classrooms. We will describe how we use these two tools flexibly to design instruction for small groups of students with similar instructional needs.

Small-Group Instruction Using Developmental Stages

Students need many models of writing to prepare them for the kinds of writing tasks that you want them to attempt. As you consider the stages that your children are in, you will design small groups in which you will model a skill or two that the students in each group need next. For example, if you have a group of students who are in the oral message category, they are using drawing as writing and making random marks, with no understanding of basic concepts about

Table 8-6. Teaching Points Based on Developmental Categories

Developmental Categories	Teaching Points
Oral Message Writer	• Copying and writing own name • Making letters • Choosing a topic • Elaborating on message • Concepts about print: left to right and top to bottom • Labeling drawings using beginning sounds
Beginning Writer	• Labeling drawings with sound-spelling • Adding details to drawing • Using mostly lowercase letters • Using finger spacing • Using the word wall • Using short-vowel sounds • Using a period at the end of a thought • Writing multiple sentences about a topic
Developing Writer	• Revising by adding on • Revising by substitution • Using long-vowel patterns • Using capital letters correctly • Using ending punctuation correctly • Using elements of a writer's craft
Experienced Writer	• Revising by moving text • Experimenting with multiple genres • Crafting piece to suit purpose • Developing an awareness of audience and voice • Organizing piece effectively

print. To prepare these students for the next stage of development, you might model how to label a few parts of a drawing, how words go from left to right, or how to develop oral language by telling about the drawing. Students in the beginning writer category would benefit from having you model adding details to a drawing, telling about the drawing, or writing a message about the drawing.

Table 8-6 illustrates the variety of teaching points for each developmental category. Our first task is to assess the developmental levels of our students, and then divide them into small groups based upon these levels. We use the information provided in this table to determine teaching points dependent on the developmental levels of the students in each group. Generally, one teaching point is enough per small-group lesson.

Small-Group Instruction Using Rubrics

We've shown you how we use rubrics to assess the needs of our students. Now we will discuss how to use those rubrics to plan for small-group instruction. We use a very simple procedure that we adapted from an idea of one of our colleagues, Deb Diller. Before beginning, you'll need to prepare a folder for use in designing your small groups. The directions are explained in Figure 8-14, and the cover is shown in Figure 8-15. On small index cards, we write four target skills found in the rubric we are currently using. We pick four skills that seem to be hardest for our students, and we write those skills on the index cards. The index cards are then slipped into the paper clips inside the writing folder, as shown in Figure 8-16.

You need: 1 file folder   razor knife
           marker   8 large paper clips
           1 library pocket

Directions:

1. Open the folder. Using the marker, draw a line down the center fold, and then another line horizontally across the middle.

2. Label the front "Small Group Writing Instruction" (see Figure 8-15).

3. Turn to the back and draw a horizontal line across the middle.

4. Glue the library pocket sideways in the bottom half of the back page (see Figure 8-18).

5. Open the folder. Using the razor knife, make 8 small slits in the folder, 2 in each section near the top, per illustration below.

6. Slide the paper clips into the slits.

Figure 8-14. Making a Folder for Small-Group Instruction

Figure 8-15. Cover of Writing Folder

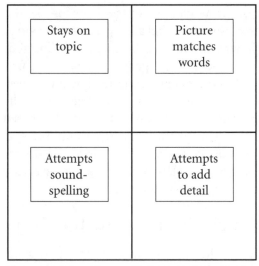

Figure 8-16. Target Skills in Writing Folder

Now that we've got our folder ready, we begin to place students in small groups. First we collect our pile of completed rubrics, some small stick-on notes, and our writing folder. For each rubric, we look at the target skill on which each student scored the lowest. If a student has the same low score on more than one target skill, we decide which target skill is more essential for that student's writing progress. We write each student's name on a stick-on note and then place the note in the section of the folder that contains the target skill on which the child needs to work. Figure 8-17 illustrates the inside of the writing folder. Ramon

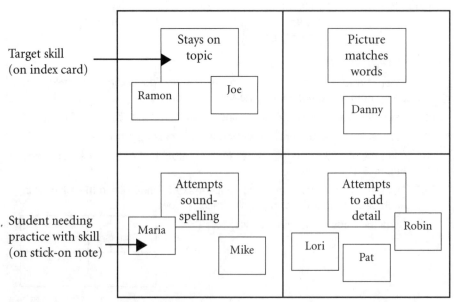

Figure 8-17. Middle of Folder

and Joe need more work on staying on topic. We need to work with Danny to help him match his pictures to his words. Maria and Mike will work with us to practice sound-spelling, and Lori, Pat, and Robin will have a small group lesson on adding details.

We find that some students don't need more work with the four target skills we've selected; instead, they need our attention in other areas. On the top half of the back of the folder, we use small stick-on notes to write these students' names and the writing skill, strategy, or technique we want to discuss with them individually. Figure 8-18 shows the back of the writing folder. Barb needs help using periods; Kelsey is experimenting with dialogue and needs some feedback; and Will needs a discussion about staying on task. At the bottom of this page, we store all of the index cards that contain our target skills so that we can reuse them.

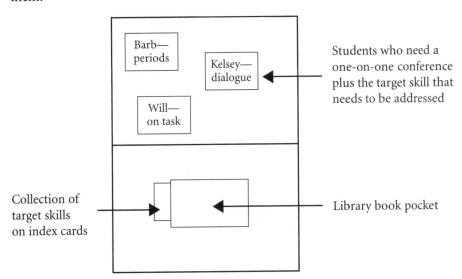

Figure 8-18.   Back of Folder

Using this arrangement, we spend a little more than 2 hours every 3 weeks or so assessing and preparing for small-group instruction. Each time we assess with rubrics, our small groups change, depending on the outcome of our assessment. Then we're prepared to use the information to teach small groups of students.

Self-Assessment

Self-assessment allows children to evaluate their own attitudes, efforts, and learning processes so that they can further their own learning. Young students aren't sophisticated when assessing their own learning, but they are capable of being honest and reflective. Johnston (1997) offers several reasons for us to value self-assessment:

- ✓ It helps students to develop independence in literacy because they don't need to rely on us for feedback.

- ✓ Self-evaluation is more immediate than having to wait for feedback from others.

- ✓ When a student discovers a problem herself, there is a greater likelihood that she will respond to it constructively.

- ✓ Students are able to intelligently discuss what they do well and what they find difficult.

- ✓ Conversations about one's own learning are productive for all members of the classroom community.

When we ask students to set their own goals for their next five-page book (as we explained in chapter 7), we are helping students to reflect on their own learning needs.

Avery (1993) offers one quick procedure for helping students to increase their self-awareness. Occasionally, at the end of writing workshop, she asks her students, "How did writing go today?" You could also ask a more specific question related to a target skill, such as "How did it go when you tried to use strong verbs?" Avery then asks her students to give her a number from 1 to 3; a 1 signifies that it was a great day for writing, 2 means okay, and 3 means that the writing didn't go well. She briefly discusses their self-evaluations, and she believes that this self-assessment is powerful. We've found that having students hold up fingers to denote their self-evaluation works well, as does having them discuss their self-assessments with a partner or in a small group.

We've also found that rubrics present a simple way to help students assess their writing progress. There is very little preparation required to convert a rubric into a form of self-assessment. We pick three or four target skills that we've been working on and create a form similar to the one in Figure 8-19. Students color the face that corresponds with their impression of their level of accomplishment. With first and second graders, it's often helpful to include a comment section with the self-assessment form. Students will often reflect more deeply about their efforts and successes if they are asked to write about it. Using a self-assessment form, students contemplate the quality of their work and are more likely to understand what they can do so their work improves.

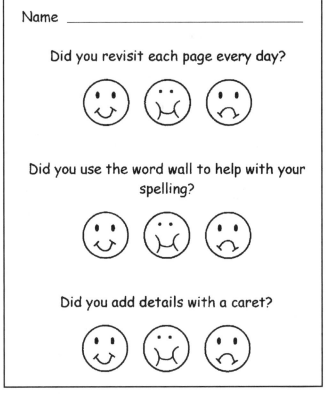

Figure 8-19.   Sample Self-Assessment Form

Utilizing Portfolios

In chapter 2, we suggested several formats for collecting student writing in portfolios. However, portfolios aren't just useful as a system for collection; they are especially valuable as you and your students look at changes over time. By examining the contents of students' portfolios, the teacher can reflect on the development, growth, and progression of their writing strengths and weaknesses (Gillespie et al., 1996). In addition, a writing portfolio is a particularly powerful tool for use during parent conferences. Parents can clearly see a child's growth and development over time. Furthermore, as students study the contents of their portfolios, they can assess their own development as a writer. In fact, "without the element of self-reflection, portfolio assessment cannot exist and the portfolio becomes just a notebook full of papers" (p. 488).

Grading Issues

It is with reluctance that we address this issue. Assessing with developmental levels and rubrics gives a much more accurate and meaningful picture of each student's successful attempts at target skills and their growth over time related to writing. These authentic types of assessment are considerably more meaningful than a grade of 83, for example, or a C–. Most teachers, however, also have to report student progress in the form of grades. Although we believe that there are better ways to report student progress, such as in the form of written narratives or personal conferences, we both are required by our districts to use grades to inform parents of each student's writing development. Instead of using an objective test that would be inadequate for our purposes, we use our writing rubrics not only to guide our instruction but to assign numerical grades as well.

Using a Rubric

We utilize a rubric rating of 0–4 on each target skill, not only to distinguish between different levels of proficiency but also to easily convert the rubric scores into numerical grades. The actual grades you assign will depend on your district's range of numbers for each grade of A, B, C, D, and F. For example, Debbie's district uses the scale of 90–100 = A; 80–89 = B; 75–79 = C; 70–74 = D; and any grade of 69 or below = U. Debbie uses this information to convert rubric scores to numerical grades using Table 8-7.

Table 8-7. Grade Conversion Chart

Rubric Score	Numerical Grade	Letter Grade
4	95	A
3	85	B
2	77	C
1	72	D
0	50	U

By following this procedure, you can use any rubric for grading purposes. However, there are still a few decisions to make. Using the sample scores in Figure 8-20, we'll discuss the grading options. One option is to add the scores and divide by 6. In this way, the student's scores are averaged, for a rubric score of 3.3. Using the grade conversion chart, we see that if a rubric score of 3 equals 85, then a score of 3.3 would be greater than 85—around a grade of 87.

Another option would be to assign grades for each target skill. In this way, we'd have six grades from the one rubric. In other words, this child would have a 95 for planning, 85 for staying on topic, 77 for adding details, and so on. A final option is to combine two or more of the rubric scores. Using the rubric in Figure 8-20, we see that the fifth and sixth target skill are related to spelling. These two scores could be combined and averaged so that we take only one grade based on spelling.

TARGET SKILLS: The writer . . .	SCORE
1. Planned 5 pages	4
2. Stayed on topic	3
3. Attempted to add details	2
4. Matched words and illustrations	4
5. Spelled word wall words correctly	3
6. Used sound-spelling to spell unfamiliar words	4

Figure 8-20. Sample Rubric Scores

Some Cautions

The example used in the preceding paragraph is an illustration only. If your district doesn't require you to use numerical or letter grades, we urge you to eliminate their use from your practice. If you must assign grades, however, you may wish to assign grades differently from the example used here. Use your professional judgment and your district's grading scale to create a grade conversion chart of your own. If you do use rubrics for grading purposes, we recommend that you don't assign numerical or letter grades for every rubric you use. You will use many rubrics only for the purposes of monitoring student progress and planning instruction.

Conclusion

Some people will read this book and perhaps say that the ideas presented within it set unrealistically high expectations for young learners. However, we know that all the ideas we suggest are achievable because we've successfully used them ourselves with primary-age children. Our students love writing. Debbie is greeted with enthusiastic anticipation when she enters a classroom to teach writing workshop. Shirl's students eagerly await writing workshop and grumble when writing time is over.

Excellence in writing takes time—time for you to become comfortable with writing instruction and time for your youngsters to grow as writers. However, with much practice, perseverance, patience, and a little passion, your young students *can* achieve the high expectations presented in this book.

One of Shirl's first graders, Gary, was struggling with reading and writing tasks. He was receiving instruction from a Reading Recovery™ teacher to improve his literacy skills. As he read an easy guided reading book, he encountered the word *crash.* Upon reading this word, Gary turned to his Reading Recovery™ teacher and said, "Hmm, onomatopoeia and a vivid verb!" Even our at-risk students can meet our high standards as they become better writers.

Throughout this book, we've shared what has worked well for us. We've tried to be as specific as possible, but we know that you will adapt our ideas to fit your students, state and district curricula, and teaching style. We've packed a lot of information into this text. Don't think that you must master all aspects right away. We suggest the following teaching sequence, taking place over the course of a year or longer, that may be useful as you plan for instruction:

1. Introduce five-page books (chapter 2) or writing journals for kindergartners (chapter 5).

2. Use target skills and did-it dots (chapter 3).

3. Begin Author's Chair routines (chapter 7).

4. Develop a system for assessment (chapter 8).

5. Begin conferences (chapter 7) and small-group instruction (chapter 8).

6. Write nonfiction books (chapter 6).

7. Implement VOICES (chapter 4).

You can visit our Web site, www.primarilywriting.com, to access necessary forms and to learn about other mini-lessons, literature connections, and teaching strategies. We both wish you good luck in your journey of raising your young writers.

Appendixes

Appendix

A

Topics Page
for Writing Folder

Topics I Can Write About

Appendix

B

Spelling Pages
for Writing Folder

Words I'm Learning to Spell	Aa	Bb
Ff	Gg	Hh
Ll	Mm	Nn
Ss	Tt	Uu

Writing Folder, page 2

Cc	Dd	Ee
Ii	Jj	Kk
Oo	Pp	Qq/Rr
Vv	Ww/Xx	Yy/Zz

Writing Folder, page 3

Appendix

C

Finished Pieces Page for Writing Folder

Books I've Written		
	Date	Title
1		
2		
3		
4		
5		
6		
7		
8		
9		
10		
11		
12		
13		
14		
15		
16		
17		
18		

Writing Folder, page 1

Appendix

Paper for
Five-Page Book

Before copying, you will need to cover this top half and the page number.

Appendix

E

Target Skills Display

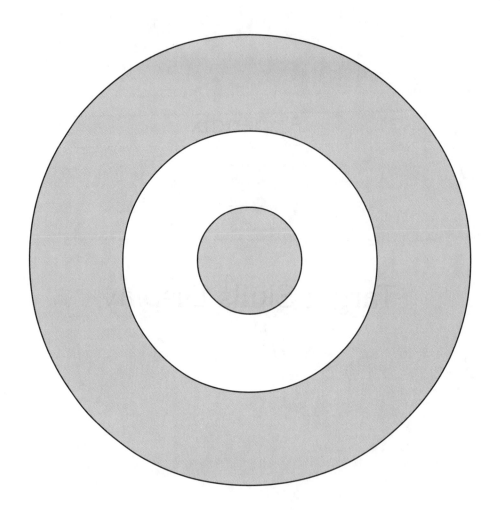

Hit the Writing
Target!

Appendix

F

Master for Target Skills

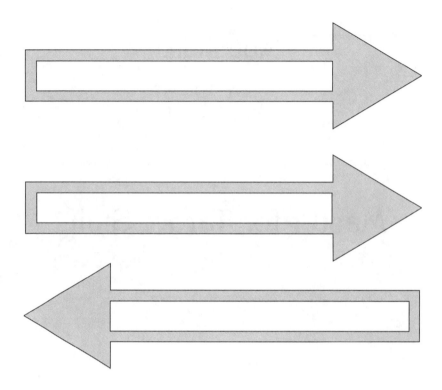

Appendix

"I've Hit the Target"
Page for Writing Folder

I've Hit the Target!	
Date	Target Skill

Writing Folder, page 5

Writing Folder, page 6

Appendix

Consult an Expert
Professional Resources

Avery, C. (1993). *And with a light touch: Learning about reading, writing, and teaching with first graders.* Portsmouth, NH: Heinemann.

Culman, R. (1998). *Picture books: An annotated bibliography with activities for teaching.* Portland, OR: Northwest Regional Educational Laboratory.

Fletcher, R. (1993). *What a writer needs.* Portsmouth, NH: Heinemann.

Fletcher, R., & Portalupi, J. (1998). *Craft lessons: Teaching writing K–8.* York, ME: Stenhouse.

McElveen, S. A., & Dierking, C. C. (Dec. 2000/Jan. 2001). Children's books as models to teach writing skills. *The Reading Teacher, 54,* 362–364.

Ray, K. W. (1999). *Wondrous words.* Urbana, IL: National Council of Teachers of English.

Routman, R. (2000). Books that encourage kids to write. In *Conversations* (pp. 126b–131b). Portsmouth, NH: Heinemann.

Spandel, V. (2001). *Creating writers through 6-trait assessment and instruction.* New York: Addison Wesley Longman.

Appendix

I

Consult an Expert
Suggested Titles

The titles are organized according to qualities of good writing (Spandel, 2001). Within each category, titles are grouped by target skill and then are alphabetized by the author's name.

Titles for Organization		
Titles	**Author**	**Target Skill**
Lilly's Purple Plastic Purse	Henkes, K.	Cause and effect
One Fine Day	Hogrogian, N.	Chain story structure
Nana Upstairs, Nana Downstairs	dePaola, T.	Chronological story structure
Why Mosquitoes Buzz in People's Ears	Aardema, V.	Cumulative story structure
If You Give a Mouse a Cookie	Numeroff, L.	Endings, Circular
The Paper Bag Princess	Munsch, R.	Endings, General

Titles for Organization *(Continued)*		
Titles	**Author**	**Target Skill**
Wilfred Gordon McDonald Partridge	Fox, M.	Endings, Poignant
Flossie and the Fox	McKissack, P.	Endings, Surprise
Miss Rumphius	Cooney, B.	Flashbacks
Millions of Cats	Gag, W.	Home-journey-home
The Art Lesson	dePaola, T.	Leads
Mirandy and Brother Wind	McKissack, P.	Leads
Tar Beach	Ringgold, F.	Leads
The Relatives Came	Rylant, C.	Leads
Sylvester and the Magic Pebble	Steig, W.	Leads
Blueberries for Sal	McCloskey, R.	Parallel plots
Whoever You Are	Fox, M.	Repeated lines
The Doorbell Rang	Hutchins, P.	Repeated lines
The Mitten	Brett, J.	Story structure
Bigmama's	Crews, D.	Story structure
Titles for Ideas		
Titles	**Author**	**Target Skill**
The Runaway Tortilla	Kimmel, E.	Adaptation of familiar tale
Little Red Cowboy Hat	Lowell, E. S.	Adaptation of familiar tale
The Frog Prince Continued	Scieszka, J.	Adaptation of familiar tale
The True Story of the Three Little Pigs	Scieszka, J.	Adaptation of familiar tale
Thinking About Ants	Brenner, B.	Combining fiction & nonfiction
The Tortilla Factory	Paulsen, G.	How to
Just Another Ordinary Day	Clement, R.	Illustrations convey information
George Shrinks	Joyce, W.	Illustrations convey information
Everett Anderson's Nine Months Long	Clifton, L.	Inner conflict
Gila Monsters Meet You at the Airport	Sharmat, M.	Inner conflict
Tell Me Again About the Night I Was Born	Curtis, J. L.	Memoir
Arthur series	Brown, M.	Moving beyond personal narrative
Chrysanthemum	Henkes, K.	Moving beyond personal narrative
Lilly's Purple Plastic Purse	Henkes, K.	Moving beyond personal narrative
Frog and Toad series	Lobel, A.	Moving beyond personal narrative
Swish!	Martin, B. M., Jr., and Sampson, M.	Narrowing a topic

Titles for Ideas (Continued)		
Titles	**Author**	**Target Skill**
The Paperboy	Pilkey, D.	Narrowing a topic
The Great Kapok Tree	Cherry, L.	Person vs. nature conflict
Just a Dream	Van Allsburg, C.	Person vs. nature conflict
The Hat	Brett, J.	Topic selection
Arthur Writes a Story	Brown, M.	Topic selection
Twinnies	Bunting, E.	Topic selection
Up North at the Cabin	Chall, M.	Topic selection
Bigmama's	Crews, D.	Topic selection
The Art Lesson	dePaola, T.	Topic selection
The Baby Sister	dePaola, T.	Topic selection
Author; A True Story	Lester, H.	Topic selection
My Rotten Red-Headed Older Brother	Polacco, P.	Topic selection
Magic Schoolbus series	Cole, J.	Topic selection; "What if" stories
Magic Treehouse series	Osborne, M. P.	"What if" stories
Titles for Word Choice		
A Walk in the Rainforest	Pratt, K. J.	Alliteration
Why Mosquitoes Buzz in People's Ears	Aardema, V.	Onomatopoeia
The Very Quiet Cricket	Carle, E.	Onomatopoeia
Mortimer	Munsch, R.	Onomatopoeia
The Listening Walk	Showers, P.	Onomatopoeia
Ordinary Things: Poems From a Walk in Early Spring	Fletcher, R.	Poetry, Language of
Honey, I Love	Greenfield, E.	Poetry, Language of
All the Small Poems	Worth, V.	Poetry, Language of
Santa Calls	Joyce, W.	Replacements for *said*
Up North at the Cabin	Chall, M. W.	Setting
The Great Kapok Tree	Cherry, L.	Setting
Miss Rumphius	Cooney, B.	Setting
Tar Beach	Ringgold, F.	Setting
My Dad	Browne, A.	Similes
Quick as a Cricket	Wood, R.	Similes
Owl Moon	Yolen, J.	Similes; vivid word choice
The Song and Dance Man	Ackerman, K.	Strong characters

Titles for Word Choice *(Continued)*		
Titles	**Author**	**Target Skill**
Miss Rumphius	Cooney, B.	Strong characters
Hey, Al	Yorinks, A.	Strong characters
Comet's Nine Lives	Brett, J.	Strong transitions
I'm in Charge of Celebrations	Baylor, B.	Strong verbs
Welcome to the Sea of Sand	Yolen, J.	Strong verbs
Everett Anderson's Goodbye	Clifton, L.	Vivid or unusual use of time
Home Place	Dragonwagon, C.	Vivid or unusual use of time
When I Was Young in the Mountains	Rylant, C.	Vivid or unusual use of time
Just a Dream	Van Allsburg, C.	Vivid or unusual use of time
Berlioz the Bear	Brett, J.	Vivid word choice
The Great Kapok Tree	Cherry, L.	Vivid word choice
Frederick	Leonni, L.	Vivid word choice
The Ghost-Eye Tree	Martin, B. M., Jr.	Vivid word choice
Listen to the Rain	Martin, B. M., Jr.	Vivid word choice
Mirandy and Brother Wind	McKissack, P.	Vivid word choice
When I Was Young in the Mountains	Rylant, C.	Vivid word choice
The Amazing Bone	Steig, W.	Vivid word choice
Sylvester and the Magic Pebble	Steig, W.	Vivid word choice

Titles for Voice	
Titles	**Author**
Where the Forest Meets the Sea	Baker, J.
A River Ran Wild	Cherry, L.
The Great Kapok Tree	Cherry, L.
Box Turtle	George, W. T.
A Little Schubert	Goffstein, M. B.
Ox-Cart Man	Hall, D.
Tight Times	Hazen, B. S.
Anniranni and Mollymishi	Lamm, C. D.
I Am the Ocean	Marshak, S.
White Dynamite and the Curly Kid	Martin, B. M., Jr., and Archambault, J.
Knots on a Counting Rope	Martin, B. M., Jr., and Archambault, J.
Hiroshima No Pika	Maruki
Farm Alphabet	Miller, J.
Junie B. Jones series	Park, B.
BUGS	Parker, N., and Wright, J.
The Keeping Quilt	Polacco, P.
Chipmunk Song	Ryder, J.
The Relatives Came	Rylant, C.
The Soda Jerk	Rylant, C.
When I Was Young in the Mountains	Rylant, C.
How Much Is a Million?	Schwartz, D. M.
The True Story of the Three Little Pigs	Scieszka, J.
Egg to Chick	Selsam, M. E.
Gila Monsters Meet You at the Airport	Sharmat, M.
Stevie	Steptoe, J.
My Special Best Words	Steptoe, J.
Early Morning in the Barn	Tafuri, N.
Nettie's Trip South	Turner, A.
I'll Fix Anthony	Viorst, J.

Appendix

J

Record-Keeping Notes

Name		
Date	Type	Notes

Types of Interactions: RC = Roving Conference; FC = Final Conference; AC = Author's Chair

Appendix

K

Target Skills
for Sharing

TARGET SKILLS FOR SHARING

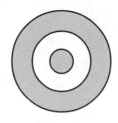

The author can set a purpose for listening.

The listener can . . .

• Summarize ▽

• Make connections ↔

• Give compliments 👍

• Help the author 💡

• Ask questions ❓

Writing Folder, page 7

Children's Books
Cited

Brett, J. (1990). *The Mitten.* New York: Putnam.

Bunting, E. (1997). *Twinnies.* New York: Harcourt Brace.

Carle, E. (1969). *The Very Hungry Caterpillar.* New York: Scholastic.

Christelow, E. (1995). *What Do Authors Do?* New York: Clarion.

Cowley, J. (1980). *Mrs. Wishy Washy.* San Diego: Wright Group.

dePaola, T. (1973). *Nana Upstairs, Nana Downstairs.* New York: Penguin Books.

dePaola, T. (1989). *The Art Lesson.* New York: PaperStar.

Fox, M. (1989). *Night Noises.* San Diego: Harcourt, Brace, Jovanovich.

Gag, W. (1928). *Millions of Cats.* Atlanta: Houghton Mifflin.

Heller, R. (1998). *Fantastic! Wow! and Unreal!: A Book About Interjections and Conjunctions.* New York: Puffin Books.

Houston, G. (1992). *My Great-Aunt Arizona.* New York: HarperCollins.

Joyce, W. (1985). *George Shrinks.* New York: Harper & Row.

Lester, H. (1997). *Author: A True Story.* Boston: Houghton Mifflin.

Lied, K. (1997). *Potato: A Tale From the Great Depression.* Washington, DC: National Geographic Society.

McKissack, P. (1986). *Flossie and the Fox.* New York: Dial Books.

Numeroff, L. (1985). *If You Give a Mouse a Cookie.* New York: Scholastic.

Pilkey, D. (1996). *The Paperboy.* New York: Orchard.

Polacco, P. (1978). *Meteor.* New York: PaperStar.

Polacco, P. (1994). *My Rotten Red-Headed Older Brother.* New York: Simon & Schuster.

Polacco, P. (1994). *Pink and Say.* New York: Philomel Books.

Polacco, P. (1998). *Thank You, Mr. Falker.* New York: Philomel Books.

Prelutsky, J. (Ed.). (1983). *The Random House Book of Poetry for Children: A Treasury of 572 Poems for Today's Child.* New York: Random House.

Ringgold, F. (1991). *Tar Beach.* New York: Crown.

Rylant, C. (1982). *When I Was Young in the Mountains.* New York: Dutton.

Rylant, C. (1985). *The Relatives Came.* New York: Bradbury.

Say, A. (1993). *Grandfather's Journey.* Boston: Houghton.

Silverstein, S. (1974). *Where the Sidewalk Ends.* New York: Harper & Row.

Soto, G. (1997). *Snapshots From the Wedding.* New York: Putnam.

Steig, W. (1969). *Sylvester and the Magic Pebble.* New York: Windmill.

Steig, W. (1976). *The Amazing Bone.* New York: Farrar.

Viorst, J. (1969). *I'll Fix Anthony.* New York: Harper & Row.

Viorst, J. (1972). *Alexander and the Terrible, Horrible, No Good, Very Bad Day.* New York: Antheneum.

Wood, A. (1982). *Quick as a Cricket.* Swindon, UK: Child's Play International.

References

Anderson, C. (2000). *How's it going?: A practical guide to conferring with student writers.* Portsmouth, NH: Heinemann.

Avery, C. (1993). *And with a light touch: Learning about reading, writing, and teaching with first graders.* Portsmouth, NH: Heinemann.

Bear, D. R., Invernizzi, M., Templeton, S., & Johnston, F. (2000). *Words their way: Word study for phonics, vocabulary, and spelling development.* Upper Saddle River, NJ: Merrill.

Calkins, L. (1986). *The art of teaching writing.* Portsmouth, NH: Heinemann.

Calkins, L. (1994). *The art of teaching writing* (2nd ed.). Portsmouth, NH: Heinemann.

Calkins, L., Montgomery, K., & Santman, D. (1998). *A teacher's guide to standardized reading tests: Knowledge is power.* Portsmouth, NH: Heinemann.

Cullinan, B. (1992). *Read to me: Raising kids who love to read.* New York: Scholastic.

Cunningham, P. (1991). *Phonics they use: Words for reading and writing.* New York: HarperCollins.

Fletcher, R. (1993). *What a writer needs.* Portsmouth, NH: Heinemann.

Fletcher, R. (1996). *A writer's notebook: Unlocking the writer within you.* New York: Avon Books.

Fletcher, R., & Portalupi, J. (1998). *Craft lessons: Teaching writing K–8.* York, ME: Stenhouse.

Freeman, M. S. (1998). *Teaching the youngest writers: A practical guide.* Gainesville, FL: Maupin House.

Gillespie, C. S., Ford, K. L., Gillespie, R. D., & Leavell, A. G. (1996). Portfolio assessment: Some questions, some answers, some recommendations. *Journal of Adolescent & Adult Literacy, 39,* (6), 480–491.

Glazer, S. M., & Brown, C. M. (1993). *Portfolios and beyond: Collaborative assessment in reading and writing.* Norwood, MA: Christopher-Gordon.

Graves, D. (1994). *A fresh look at writing.* Portsmouth, NH: Heinemann.

Harvey, S., & Goudvis, A. (2000). *Strategies that work: Teaching comprehension to enhance understanding.* York, ME: Stenhouse.

Johnson, B. (1999). *Never too early to write: Adventures in the K–1 writing workshop.* Gainesville, FL: Maupin House.

Johnston, P. H. (1997). *Knowing literacy: Constructive literacy assessment.* York, ME: Stenhouse.

Miller, D. (2002). *Reading with meaning: Teaching comprehension in the primary grades.* Portland, ME: Stenhouse.

Moline, S. (1995). *I see what you mean: Children at work with visual information.* York, ME: Stenhouse.

Parkes, B. (2000). *Read it again!: Revisiting shared reading.* Portland, ME: Stenhouse.

Pearson, P. D., & Gallagher, M. C. (1983). The instruction of reading comprehension. *Contemporary Educational Psychology, 8,* 317–344.

Ray, K. W. (1999). *Wondrous words.* Urbana, IL: National Council of Teachers of English.

Rickards, D., & Cheek, E. (1999). *Designing rubrics for K–6 classroom assessment.* Norwood, MA: Christopher-Gordon.

Routman, R. (1991). *Invitations: Changing as teachers and learners K–12.* Portsmouth, NH: Heinemann.

Routman, R. (2000). *Conversations.* Portsmouth, NH: Heinemann.

Snowball, D. (1995, May). Building literacy skills through nonfiction: Some tips on how you can help children become better readers and writers of nonfiction. *Teaching K–8, 62–63.*

Spandel, V. (2001). *Creating writers through 6-trait assessment and instruction.* New York: Addison Wesley Longman.

Taberski, S. (2000). *On solid ground: strategies for teaching reading K–3.* Portsmouth, NH: Heinemann.

Tannenbaum, J. (2000). *Teeth, wiggly as earthquakes: Writing poetry in the primary grades.* York, ME: Stenhouse.

Teale, W. (1995). Dear readers. *Language Arts, 72,* 80.

Vacca, R. T., & Vacca, J. L. (1999). *Content area reading: Literacy and learning across the curriculum.* New York: Longman.

Zemelman, S., Daniels, H., & Hyde, A. (1993). *Best practice: New standards for teaching and learning in America's schools.* Portsmouth, NH: Heinemann.

About the Authors

Debbie Rickards is the literacy support specialist at Boone Elementary in the Alief Independent School District in Houston, Texas. She has taught in the elementary grades for over twenty-five years, and also teaches graduate level literacy classes for the University of St. Thomas in Houston. She is author, with Earl Cheek, Jr., of *Designing Rubrics for K-6 Classroom Assessment* from Christopher-Gordon Publishers. She received her Ph.D. from Louisiana State University in 1997.

Shirl Hawes is a Reading Recovery and first grade teacher at Drabek Elementary in the Fort Bend Independent School District in Houston, Texas. She has taught primary grades for over twenty years in school districts across Texas. She is the author, with Laurie MacGillivray, of "'I Don't Know What I'm Doing – They All Start with B': First Graders Negotiate Peer Reading Interactions" published in *The Reading Teacher* in November 1994. She is a 2001 recipient of the Fulbright Memorial Fund Teacher Scholarship for study in Japan.

Index